Soulfully ablaze

Soulfully ablaze

A 40-DAY JOURNEY TO LIGHT UP YOUR LIFE (AND THE WORLD)

SARAH DAVISON-TRACY

IGNITE!
PUBLISHERS

Soulfully Ablaze: A 40-Day Journey to Light Up Your Life (And the World)

Published by Ignite Publishers
Denver, CO

Library of Congress Control Number: 2018903969
DAVISON-TRACY, SARAH, Author
Soulfully Ablaze
Sarah Davison-Tracy

ISBN: 978-0-9997212-1-6

BODY, MIND & SPIRIT / Inspiration & Personal Growth
SELF-HELP / Personal Growth / General
PHILOSOPHY / Movements / Idealism

COVER DESIGN: ASTRID KOCH

AUTHOR PHOTO: J RENAE DAVIDSON

INTERIOR LAYOUT: ANDREA COSTANTINE

QUANTITY PURCHASES: Schools, companies, professional groups, clubs, and other organizations may qualify for special terms when ordering quantities of this title. For information, email Info@IgnitePublishers.com.

IGNITE!
PUBLISHERS

● ● ●

To the One whose Love planted the seeds of this story in my heart
... this work is all Yours—I am all Yours.

To my *kula*, my community for life
... this book has emerged from and for you.
Without you, this story could not have been crafted.

xo
Sarah DT

Contents

Contents

BE BOLD. BE BRAVE. BE YOU.

[we begin]

Greetings, my friend.
This is your tour guide speaking.

Wherever you find yourself at this moment
—excited, stressed, curious, tired—
I invite you to settle in, buckle up, and hold on,
because we are going for a ride.

You will not be bored on this road trip.
This is no ho-hum *jOURney*.

These days together will kindle and awaken,
such that by the end, you are different,
seeing yourself and the world anew.

Welcome

DEAR FRIEND, WELCOME. I'VE BEEN EXPECTING AND PREPARING FOR YOU TO ARRIVE FOR QUITE SOME TIME. I'M *SO GLAD* YOU ARE HERE. THIS IS NO ACCIDENT THAT TODAY IS THE DAY TO BEGIN. THIS IS DESTINY.

The forty-day journey ahead is a radically simple—simply radical— way to fuel your life, still the noise, and discover your next steps, allowing you to connect more with yourself and others as you go. It promises to provide you with deeper meaning in every aspect of your life.

This journey builds deep strength within and cultivates a greater-than-ever capacity to act with boldness, bravery, and inspiration, no matter what life brings. Along the way, you'll find that there are many kindred others traveling with you and you'll feel less alone. Throughout this journey, you will weave soulful learnings and practices into more bits of your life in ways that will create *plentiful peace, flourishing freedom, herculean hope, and limitless love.*

You may be wondering, "Why should I go?" "What is the cost?" "What can I expect?" "When does it begin?" Indeed, these are important considerations for the road. So, my friend, let's pour ourselves a virtual cup of tea and settle in. We'll move through each one of these thoughtful queries together.

Why Should I Go?

THIS JOURNEY WILL UNLEASH WITHIN YOU A NEW VISION FOR YOUR UNIQUE WAYS TO BE A VITAL PART OF THE LIVES OF THOSE WHO MATTER MOST TO YOU IN YOUR FAMILY, NEIGHBORHOOD, AND IN FAR-FLUNG PARTS OF THE WORLD.

It will amplify your purpose on the planet and help you cultivate a tribe of people that will delight and surprise you. It will fan the flame of your dormant or blazing dreams. One step at a time, your life will begin to light up with an unmistakable glow.

This journey includes sojourns on the road—beautiful and restorative resting places to cultivate energy to emerge up and out of the soil. These regular rhythms of pausing and tending to what your body, mind, and soul are clamoring for will bear great and surprising gifts.

This journey is profound. It will meet you just where you are. You will listen to and look for nudges rooted in wisdom and the realities of your life *here and now*. You will start where you are and work with what you have. Whether you're worn out from operating for too long in service and action without a moment to catch your breath, or you've been too long stuck and stationary, you will discover just what you need in here. You will discover and deepen your sense of security and peace, even when your way seems murky, unclear, and when life is just plain hard.

This journey will reveal your ever-unfolding story and next steps. Breakthrough and epiphany reside here. Watch for it. Count on it.

This is where the fire of your life is *stoked*.

> This journey will reveal your ever-unfolding story and next steps. Breakthrough and epiphany reside here. Watch for it. Count on it.

What Can I Expect?

FORTY POPS (PLACES OF PAUSE) ARE AT THE CORE OF THIS JOURNEY. THESE POPS ARE ESSENTIAL.

Each of the PoPs has three parts: *Be Still*, *Ponder*, and *Engage*. Collectively, they are opportunities for contemplation and action.

The times to *Be Still* and *Ponder* are all about intention and attention. Refreshment is found here. They offer moments to cultivate discernment, thoughtful planning, and momentum for change. Your inspiration to *Engage* will be rooted in the stability and wisdom you cultivate in stillness and pondering, free of the frantic or forceful energy that often accompanies quests for transformation. You may find yourself inspired to act in big or small, local or global ways. Whatever the scale, the locale, and the perceived impact, what comes to you will be *life-changing, peace-making, bridge-building,* and *change-making.*

You can use this book on its own or as a companion to *Live Ablaze: And Light Up the World.* Each of the *Ablaze* books provides distinct experiences. Both books are all about you. Both are *about setting your* life ablaze with more than you have dared to *dream about,* think of, or imagine. Both are about living life with more riveting connection within yourself and with others. And yet, the spotlight in *Soulfully Ablaze* is even more deeply focused on you, with shorter stories about others excerpted from *Live Ablaze,* providing ample space for you to deepen and cultivate your journey through the forty Places of Pause (PoPs).

The world gives itself up to incessant activity merely because it knows of nothing better. The inspired man works among its whirring wheels also, but he knows whither the wheels are going. For he has found the centre where all is stillness...
-Paul Brunton

The Three Elements of pops

MY FRIEND, LET'S TAKE A DEEPER LOOK AT EACH OF THE ELEMENTS OF OUR POPS.

1st ... Be Still

It's one of those simple, but often not easy, things to do. Here, you will take time to stop. To breathe. To take a moment to do nothing. It may be ten seconds or ten minutes. But, for many of us, it may be ten seconds or ten minutes longer than we typically allow ourselves. This moment to *Be Still* may feel exceedingly uncomfortable or profoundly peaceful … or somewhere in between.

If you are able, before this time to *Be Still*, carve out an additional minute or two to pour yourself a glass of something cool and refreshing or warm and cozy to enjoy. Light a candle to bring a bit of beauty to your day, as a symbol of the fire you are stoking in your journey, or as a bit of good juju for someone in your life in need of a spark of light and hope.

There is a simple free verse reading to set up each nudge to *Be Still* that includes bits of surrender and invitations to cultivate silence and quiet. As you slow down, you may discover that you need a bit of extra rest. If so—and if you can make it happen now, later, or tomorrow—take a moment. Lie down. Even if you only have one, five, or ten minutes to shut your eyes, do it. Set your timer and take a breather.

2nd ... Ponder

Before you plow forward into the time of *soulFULL* reflection, hold off on pulling out that journal just yet. Scan yourself, gently and intently. Ask: *What do I need or want? What would feel good today, in this very moment?* Allow what you need from day to day to change.

One day, you may want to record your impressions, thoughts, and feelings into a voice memo on your phone ... another day you may want to draw and/or write. At times, you may want to step outside for a walk, in silence and solitude, taking one of the section's questions along with you for consideration. As you go, breathe deeply, feel the fresh air on your skin, and be surprised and delighted by what comes to you as you walk.

You'll find that I've included a song at each place of pondering, to share with you some musical artistry and beauty. See what you love (or don't) in the words, the harmonies, and the rhythms. Put on your headphones and walk around the block with the song as your companion, get up and dance, or sit down and let the music wash over you. If you don't dig my jams, not to worry. I get it. Music is a deeply personal preference—maybe you'll choose to create your own PoP mix of inspiration that you love.

As you respond to the inquiries in this *Ponder* moment of the PoPs, imagine and articulate as many details as you possibly can. Get specific. Be creative. Be honest. Feel free to respond to each of the questions, a few of them, or none at all.

However you choose to enter into the prompts to *Ponder*, these moments will form and inform the roots you are creating, so that you flourish ... deeply and wholeheartedly. Here, you will tend to your heart's desires, longings, and needs. You will cultivate and uncover inspiration, direction, *enCOURAGEment*, and energy for the days to come.

These moments will form and inform the roots you are creating, so that you flourish ... deeply and wholeheartedly.

3rd ... Engage

This third, more active element generates mighty momentum and direction for your life. You will have the opportunity to choose what you want to do. What or who are you beckoned to *commit to, connect with*, or *create*—whether in small or big ways? These elements of inspired action will clarify, strengthen, and more deeply root some of the ideas percolating within you.

This is a place to play, to experiment, to explore in the midst of the realities of your life here and now. These will be catalysts for what might come next for you—possibly something that appears *big*, like writing a book, making a film, quitting your job or starting a new one, volunteering, or taking a service-exchange trip. Or maybe it doesn't look *big*, but it changes your day-to-day—how you walk through life, think about and treat those nearest to you, and see your part in the world.

This is about bit-by-bit, step-by-step, leap-by-leap living into extravagant love, jaw-dropping creativity, not-yet-seen innovation, and small, medium, or large actions. These inspired actions will, over time, change your life and bring change to the world. You will do good and feel better than ever.

Each PoP ends with a one-word reflection. You'll see this image, a cairn. In the bottom of the stack of rocks, write a word that reflects what is capturing your attention during each PoP. This is a way to simply refine into some gold, as a result of each PoP, a bunch of ideas, opportunities, and feelings.

These one-word reflections open you up to a creative and dynamic way to grow and learn, cultivate clarity and focus, and engage and wake up your brain. Over time, these one-word reflections of your PoPs will create a snapshot of what matters most to you. They will become an archive of your story.

> This is about bit-by-bit, step-by-step, leap-by-leap living into extravagant love, jaw-dropping creativity, not-yet-seen innovation, and small, medium, or large actions. These inspired actions will, over time, change your life and bring change to the world. You will do good and feel better than ever.

When Does It Start & End?

CONSIDER MOVING THROUGH THE POPS AS A FORTY-DAY EXPERIENCE, LIVING WITH EACH POP FOR A DAY.

The timeframe of a forty-day journey is rooted in the power of both the spiritual and scientific to notably *reframe, restart,* and *regenerate.* As you go, you'll actually be making brand new neural pathways in your brain. (And how amazing is that?)

Research in the field of neurosciece has proven that after just thirty days of repetition, a practice becomes effortless. It becomes a habit. A new route in the brain has been forged. In the spiritual arena, forty days is a sacred time period that is found across many of the world's religions, marking many rites of passage around the globe related to birth, death, and transition. This journey has some strong roots and it will cultivate the same strength in you.

The final chapter "Taking Flight" is a celebration of your forty-day journey. From that vantage point, you'll get a *panoramic view* of your path to discern the gold that has emerged in your life. If you choose to move through this chapter as a continuation of your forty-day journey, might you set aside a few extra hours to move through this final chapter? You may need to break it down into a few days, which will also work beautifully. See what works for you. Either way, think of this final chapter as a simple and soulful private retreat with a bit of a *rollicking finale.*

The timeframe of a forty-day journey is rooted in the power of both the spiritual and scientific to notably *reframe, restart, and regenerate.*

How Might I Create a Daily Rhythm?

IN LATIN, THE WORD FOR *JOURNEY* IS "DIURNUS," MEANING "OF A DAY OR DAILY."

So, my friend, I invite you to explore ways to integrate this journey of forty PoPs into a daily practice, or even a practice you enter into a few times throughout the day.

For a glimpse at how these rhythms of PoPs look in my everyday life, I start my mornings with a PoP that always involves a steaming cup of coffee, a lit candle, my journal, and my sacred text, the Bible, while the house is quiet and before I jump into the day's demands. Sometimes it's ten minutes; sometimes it's an hour. At midday, I pause for another PoP, and I head outside for a few minutes to take in some fresh air or read something that inspires me. (This one takes the most discipline for me to honor, and yet, it never fails to refresh me.) At night, before I go to sleep, I take a final PoP to review my day and prepare for the day ahead, paying attention to any niggling bits of worry or unresolved challenges, and surrender them to the Sacred. I always end with one or two things to be grateful for. These PoPs are done within the context of a full-to-the-brim life of family, work, vacation, sickness, the unplanned and unexpected, the minutia of to-dos. They bookend and fuel my days.

It may take a few days or weeks to settle into your personal feel-good rhythm of PoPs—or you may find it right away. As you create your daily rhythm of quiet time to *Be Still*, *Ponder*, and *Engage*, fueled by *soulFULL* insight and inspiration, watch for game-changing ripples in your life.

As you create your daily rhythm of quiet time to Be Still, Ponder, and Engage, fueled by soulFULL insight and inspiration, watch for game-changing ripples in your life.

How Much Does It Cost?

LIFE IS NOT EASY. THIS JOURNEY IS ROOTED IN THE REAL, THE RAW, THE NITTY-GRITTY REALITIES OF BEING HUMAN. SO, IT'S NOT EASY. BUT, IT IS SO *GOOD*.

I have a hunch it will awaken and set your heart ablaze. When it does, a life of palpable purpose and one-of-a-kind destiny will be yours. You will experience peace, ease, grace, passion, and joy to your very core. Love will pulse in you, as effortlessly as the thrum-thrum of your heart.

It may be daunting to set off on a journey of exploration for your purpose on the planet. It may be demanding to consider the nudge to connect more deeply with your global human family—whether near or far. Listening, tending to, and responding to this journey may disrupt and ruffle some feathers.

The cost will vary—depending on where this journey finds you in your life at this very moment. It may be challenging and costly to block out a few minutes every day and stick to it for forty days. No doubt, your life is full to the brim and your bandwidth may seem at an all-time low. But, the lower the bandwidth and the greater the overwhelm, isolation, and doubt within you, the greater the need for this journey.

Struggle and pain abound, whether in the lives of those you love or in the greater world *out there*. The bigger the pain, the more we need these PoPs. You may be knee deep, feeling as though you're treading water in your care of children, parents, friends, or work. (My friend, kudos—big kudos—for all that you do every day to keep going … especially on the really hard days.) The more you have to do and the more you are committed to caring for others, the more essential are these PoPs. Responding frantically and reactively to each and every need that comes your way can burn you out and leave you running on fumes. If you are deafened by a plethora of needs clam-

In the midst of the raw and real challenges and joys of life, no matter what season of life you are in, these places of pausing, of pondering, of wise and inspired engagement offer potent fuel for your life … for you.

oring for your attention in your family, work, or in the world, carving out this time for a forty-day journey will be a well-deserved gift.

Even if you are rock solid and crystal clear about your purpose on the planet, your life's *why*, and the *who* you are committed to serve, practicing these PoPs daily will energize you. Doing so will cultivate fuel for your heart's compassionate pulse, illumination and discernment of your next steps, and knowledge that your worth is not tied to your external success and performance.

In the midst of the raw and real challenges and joys of life, no matter what season of life you are in, these places of pausing, of pondering, of wise and inspired engagement offer potent fuel for your life … for you.

Love will pulse in you, as effortlessly as the thrum-thrum of your heart.

your pop plan

WHAT MIGHT YOUR FORTY-DAY POP JOURNEY LOOK LIKE?

How much time can you set aside each day for your PoPs?

If you are able, try to keep it to the same time of day. Scan your days for even a pocket of time that you can carve out and commit to. Don't put this off for later when you will be less busy or have more energy. Start with what you have and where you are right now. If you miss a day, not to worry—just pick up the PoPs the next day. Keep it simple, my friend.

As we continue on this journey, my friend,
may your life become
more than you thought to ask for or imagine,
with a spring in your step you didn't have before.

In the forty days to come,
may you find more of your own story
and discover and experience
that,
together,
we are mighty.

1

[kindling]

exciting. stirring up. starting a fire
animating. rousing. inflaming lighting
up. illuminating. making bright.

Open your heart and mind to the purpose pulsating within you.
What is a desire of your heart that will take your breath away?
Yeah … that one.

The one that is calling,
summoning you to say yes, to act, to step out,
and to *COURAGEously* claim that this is the time.

Invite in the sort of love that propels and *emBOLDens* bravery.
If fear pipes up, tell it to take a back seat;
turn down the volume of its clamor.

You are here with a breathtaking destiny.
Dreams have been planted in you
and they beckon for your attention.
As you tend to them, they will
grow, get stronger, awaken, and nudge you
to open and deepen your connection
within you
and with your mighty human family—near and far.

what's possible for you

You are what the world has been waiting for
in all your real-ness and splendor-ness.
Sometimes all it takes is a bit of fuel to get
that fire going.

In the economy of love's ways,
there is always plenty.
With love as the fuel for who you are
and for what you do,
you are more than enough.

Your dreams and desires are
where your vision, your what,
and your why are planted,
where you come alive and where
the crescendo of your life is fueled.
Your purpose on the planet is rooted here.

The time is now to kindle your dreams
—whether brand new or old—
and strengthen your heart
to believe that the time is now.
As you do, get ready for the sonic boom
that will set your life aglow.

Limitless Love

LOVE. IT IS A TRAVEL ESSENTIAL ON THIS ROAD TO ALL THAT IS POSSIBLE.

The lens of limitless love allows you to see your next steps and leaps that will lead toward your big dreams and unique inspired purpose on the planet—in your backyard and in distant lands.

Limitless love invites you to live *BEloved*.

Living *BEloved* fuels you to be love. Always. Not always immediately, but *always*. It knows when you've been strengthened enough and have filled up enough to be ready for the delight of being love to those around you. It is not a burdensome doing; it is like a dance, like a song, and it is joyful. When this plentiful love is the primary fuel for who you are and what you do, your passion, strength, and courage will be more than enough. Always enough. In the economy of love's ways, there is perpetually plenty.

Do you hear it? No?
Then, I will whisper it.
You are loved.
Like crazily, over-the-top-ly, fully.
Always have been. Always will be.
Loved. Celebrated. Cherished. *DeLIGHTed* in.
You are loved, *BEloved*.
Take it in. Inhale it.
Let it take root. Flourish.
The courtroom—
judgments and words of too much/not enough,
good/bad, beautiful/ugly—
is adjourned.
Over. Now. Today, tomorrow, and the next day.
All the days from now to infinity.

Perhaps here people are materially well off, but I think if we looked inside the houses we should find that it is difficult sometimes to smile at each other, even though such a smile might be the beginning of love. For this reason, we always greet each other with a smile, because it is the beginning of love, and when one begins to love it is natural to want to do something.
-Mother Teresa, *Mother Teresa: Her Life Her Works*

Welcome, to our first place of pause, of sojourn. Don't rush by this part. It's so good and so important. Consider pouring yourself a glass of something deliciously icy or steaming and comfy. Take care of yourself. Light a candle for the pure beauty of it or as a picture of kindling, of getting the fire going.

Be Still (surrender)

I invite you to take a breath.
Another one … deeper still.
Now, my friend, pause.
Before you consider anything:
actions or ideas that inspire,
needs or worries that burden,
here and now, take another deep breath.

Idle here for a moment longer.
Hold off on the to-dos, the what-ifs.
And linger in the exquisiteness of *BEing*.

Sit for ten seconds or ten minutes.
Just be.

ponder (go deeper)

After reading through the questions below, consider how you want to reflect and voice your thoughts. Is it in a journal, in a voice memo, in a totally different way, unique to you? Move through these ponderings freely, without thinking too deeply about each or trying to force ideas or answers. If you prefer, head out for a walk with one of the questions from the list below in your mind. EnJOY nature's warmth or coolness, lightness or darkness.

Now or later, as you go about your day, listen (and watch the video, if you can) to this song, one of my favorites of all time: "Glow," sung by Donavan Frankenreiter. Dear friend, let's glow, love, and fly together.

What do you think would change in you if you allowed yourself, your thoughts, and your actions to be fueled more by this big, epic, plentiful love of living *BEloved*? What would you do more or less of? What would be different?

Pick one phrase or sentence that captured your attention in the reading above and write a bit about it. How does it connect with your life, right here and now? Is there a gem in it for you to chew on and sit with for a bit?

Engage (commit)

A nudge. Consider how the idea of this active way to *be love* would fuel you anew today or this week. Identify one person, near or far, who comes to mind—someone who could use a dose of this big love. Allow this person to be you, if you need to gently care for yourself today. Does an inspired action bubble up? Might you send a text or email, do something little or big for this someone?

Now, it's your turn. What or who are you beckoned to *commit to, connect with,* or *create*—whether in small or big ways?

Share something from this PoP with someone you trust.

Your Word. Write a word that has captured your attention in this PoP.

BE BOLD. BE BRAVE. BE YOU.

Dreams & Desires

WHEN YOU DREAM BIG, YOU ARE AWAKE.
YOU ARE STRONG AND FIERCE.

**You hold your head high; your eyes are direct and focused.
You speak clearly about what matters to you.**

You keep it real, and you look for and find the same in others. You are at peace among the oft' present imperfections, discomfort, and unknown. Fog and confusion lessen … and they don't matter so much when they do come into view. You listen and act with conviction and inspiration. You discover that the things that have separated you from yourself and others decrease. The ways you think and talk about what matters in life is captivating and expansive.

Tending to and fanning the flames of your dreams and desires are some of the starting points for our *jOURney*. Look for them. Explore them. Trust them, my friend. Yes, trust them, whether itty-bitty or whopping dreams. They offer some clues for your unfolding story.

And, my friend, share them, too. Yes, your dreams are meant to be shared. They rarely grow when kept inside you. They need to be brought out into the open, to be spoken, to be exposed to the light of day and the real in the world. Sharing your dreams can be daunting and leave you feeling vulnerable, and yet, what happens as a result of sharing them is pure magic. *You will be lit up.*

It may feel as though your dreams are dormant. You may have become disconnected from your sense of your palpable purpose. Or maybe you don't see a way to connect those dreams with your everyday life. Not to worry. They are with you right now. They may just need a bit of nurturing, of gentle encouragement to c'mon out. In Nepal, they have a word I love, particularly when it comes to things like this that cannot be rushed

Let yourself be drawn by the pull of what you really love.
-Rumi

or forced. It is *bistari*, which means "slowly." *Bistari* gives us permission to move gently, intentionally, and without rushing.

My friend, whether you have a hunch,
no idea at all, or laser clarity about your small or big dreams,
I'm cheering you on.
Wherever you find yourself right here and now
is good—it is plenty.
More will be discovered and uncovered
in the days to come.
Bistari.

Be Still (surrender)

Take a breath.
Another one.
Soften your face.
Close your eyes.

Whether you feel the kindling of an old dream,
the pulsing possibility of a new one,
or the disappointment of seemingly dormant dreams,
let it all go.
Those are all important things,
but they can be tended to later.
Here and now, it is about stillness and silence.
Peace to your heart, your mind, your soul.
Just be
for this moment.
Stay here for ten seconds or ten minutes.

ponder (go deeper)

Listen to the song, "Dreams," sung by The Cranberries. Get up and out of your seat and sing, dance, spin, jump around. Go for a walk, dare to dance a bit as you go.

Fan the flame of your itty bitty or supersized dream. Write some more. Even if you see it faintly, write about what you see, what you feel. If you removed any goals or measurables, such as making an impact, making a difference, or even making money, what do you dream of having time to do more of? What would be just plain amazing to do more of in life? Play and frolic in your imagination.

Are you drawn in by *bistari*? What would it be like to claim, "I am not in a rush" just for this moment, to embrace *bistari*? Breathe it. Sit with it. What if even in the midst of big dreams, big vision, big hope, big destiny, you embrace not needing to rush, to do anything just now? Or, have you been moving in *bistari* for too long and are now ready to speed things up a bit? How might you begin to move in a way that energizes you?

Can you see, taste, and feel your dream? If it were a seed or something growing, what might that look like? Is it underground? Does it have small or big roots? Has the growth popped up above the soil? Is it clamoring for your attention—does it need water or fertilizer or more sunlight? Is it begging you for some space to grow, weeding out the competing weeds that are choking it? Draw it. Write about it and describe it. Or hold it close to your heart and in your thoughts as you sit or walk for a few moments.

Engage (commit)

A nudge: If you sense the need for more *bistari*, choose a time and place to move slowly today, in your everyday, real life … whether for a minute or an hour. Make it a specific time (for instance, in your car for one minute before heading in for work) or activity (maybe lunch today—eat where you want, while reading a book, sitting in the sun, with some new act of *bistari*). As you do, note how you feel, what you're thinking. Pay attention to the gold in you.

Now, it's your turn. What or who are you beckoned to *commit to*, *connect with*, or *create*—whether in small or big ways?

Share something from this PoP with someone you trust.

Your Word. Write a word that has captured your attention in this PoP.

BE BOLD. BE BRAVE. BE YOU.

Here Comes The Boom!

WHEN I FIND MYSELF IN A DREAMLESS STATE OR A PLACE OF DRIP-DROP DREAMS, I PLAY IT SAFE.

I hide and isolate myself from my trusted tribe, those who inspire and support me. Fear takes hold and courage—whoosh—is gone.

Day-to-day endeavors become laborious and heavy. Work is hard—too hard. I might be doing lots of good stuff, but the *DOing* is forced and compressed. It seems there is not enough of me, of time, of anything.

Can you relate? Have you forgotten to dream or are you dreaming small—drip-drop—dreams? Are you too often alone and isolated? Is the everyday *DOing* in your life just plain hard? Have you been playing it a bit too safe, or have you been afraid to move in any direction?

If you have been living in a less-than-you way, step out of the shadows and drop your strenuous doing. C'mon out. It's time for some good news. Are you ready? Here comes the *boom*!

Dream big.
Start small.
But most of
all, start.
-Simon Sinek

The time is now to kindle your dreams. You need not try harder. You only need to patiently and fervently trust that where you are is just right. Each and every step of the way, you have been mysteriously and dynamically prepared by your own heart, by life, and by those around you to be where you are right now on this *jOURney*.

Wherever you are, whatever you're doing, imagine what your dream looks and feels like. Your dreams and desires are being lit up. Get ready for the *Boom!* of what will happen as it kindles.

Start here and now, right where you are,
whether in the carpool line;
at home doing laundry;
at your office or shop;
driving a cab, tuck-tuck, or rickshaw;
making pasta, samosas, posh, or arapas;
caring for young children or elderly parents;
entering college or starting a new career in the middle of life;
loving work or hating it; hopeful or hopeless.
You were made for this.
You're not alone.
Trust.
Hope.

Be Still (surrender)

Surrender. Silence. Stillness.
Breathe.
Take some long, deep breaths.
Relax your muscles from the tip of your head to your toes.
Enjoy being, just being, for a few moments.
Stop moving, racing, thinking, planning.
Stay here for ten seconds or ten minutes.

ponder (go deeper)

Listen to the song, "Go," sung by Sandra McCracken. Fellas, swap out the female pronouns for your own … you are part of this story too. Imagine the places to which you are being drawn, the parts of life that are becoming more clear, and consider if you are ready to *go*. Listen for and watch the doubt and the noises becoming quieter. *Ahh.* Write about what comes to you.

What phrases or images struck you as you read this chapter? These are crumbs and clues for the road ahead, meant just for you. Sit with them. Explore what connections there are in your life today to these morsels of insight.

What comes to you as you consider your drip-drop dreams and desires? Do you see a small dream that might grow, bit by bit, into a bigger, perhaps even an oceanic, one? Have you been living in a smaller-than-is-really-you vision of yourself? Where in your life, in your dreams, would you like a *Boom!* of ignition?

Engage (commit)

A nudge. Do one thing today for the pure joy of it, with no anticipated outcome other than your enjoyment. Whether it's what you eat, listen to, watch, do, or who you spend time with ... this is all about connecting with your heart's desire, your longing in an every-day way. *This* is kindling your dreams.

Now, it's your turn. What or who are you beckoned to *commit to, connect with*, or *create*—whether in small or big ways?

Share something from this PoP with someone you trust.

Your Word. Write a word that has captured your attention in this PoP.

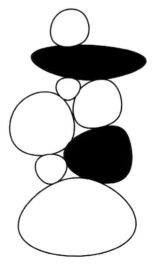

BE BOLD. BE BRAVE. BE YOU.

unstoppable

You are destined for more than
you can be and do on your own.
Individually, you are extraordinary,
with great capacity and power.
Yup, you rock.

And ... there's more.
When you open your heart and mind
to the people around you,
to those in your mighty human family
—strangers and friends alike—
you will discover possibilities,
joy, and strength
in surprising places.

Humbly and WHOLEheartedly,
see and welcome others into your story,
and invite them to share their own.

Together, life is better.
Infinitely more is possible.
You—we—are unstoppable.

Vital Tribe

WHETHER I FEEL GOOD OR BAD, STRONG OR WEAK, ON TOP OF THE WORLD, OR AT ROCK BOTTOM, I HAVE EXPERIENCED OVER AND OVER WHAT HAPPENS WITH MY TRIBE. IT'S MAGIC.

It's breathtaking. It's real. It's game-changing and difference-making. This tribe I speak of is composed of a vital three-part collective without whom I cannot imagine navigating life—from dealing with the day-to-day minutia, to epic leaps of courage, to going after big dreams. Each one matters greatly.

First and foremost is my relationship with the Sacred, who is with me—present, persistent, and pervading—in every single bit of life, no matter the content or context: relational or vocational, healing or heartbreaking, messy or clear, hopeful or hopeless. Everything begins, is sustained, and ends here in my life. The second element of my tribe is my trusted soul friends, with whom I grow and to whom I am committed to share all of me … my highest hopes and greatest foibles. The third aspect is comprised of those I don't yet know—"strangers," for now—in my human family, but with whom there is a growing sense of being more inextricably interconnected each day. They are the ones who inspire and fuel my purpose and passions on a daily basis.

Kula is an ancient Sanskrit word, which means "community of the heart." Your purpose on the planet—big or small in impact, local or global—is not about carving something out alone; it only happens within a *kula*. The people with whom you want to travel through life may look very different from mine. No doubt, your collective will have a unique flavor. But, no matter how it looks, it must not be a *kula* of one, in which you are doing life by yourself.

Your plane will be grounded and your wheels harnessed to the cement if you try to go it alone. To those of you who think you can fly solo, I double-dog-dare you to see where this journey with others takes you. The good news about this adventure is that with a community of support, you will create a richer, more vibrant support system than ever that will enCOURAGE you to *be bold, be brave, and be you.*

May this notion of one's *kula* as vital
deeply permeate your days.

The *EVERYday* is important because
it is where you spend most of your life.
And when the passion, energy, and rhythms
of this day-to-day are lit up and fueled,
life is good.

This is an ordinary and extraordinary tribe:
soul friends, a growing global human family, and the Sacred.
It is one that is here with and for you in it all:
when you get a promotion, while you're on vacation,
as you do laundry, cook dinner, or
find yourself in a disagreement with someone you love,
in the midst of addiction,
when you are in a quandary about what to do next,
fully expressing or hiding big bits of yourself,
at rock bottom or ecstatic about life.

Let's keep walking,
putting one foot in front of the other,
together.

Be Still (surrender)

What do you need today in this time of *BEing*?
What do you need to let go of, surrender?
If you see it and know it, imagine handing it off
or see it floating away on the clouds.
If you don't know what to surrender just now,
imagine your next exhale releasing what burdens you.
Inhale deeply.
Exhale completely.

Close your eyes.
Breathe.
Take ten seconds or minutes to be.

ponder (go deeper)

Before you dive in...do you want to take one of these questions with you on a walk? Do you have time to make a cup of tea or a refreshing icy drink? Wherever you are, consider how you can make this moment just right for you.

Listen to "Better Together," sung by Jack Johnson. Write about what comes to you, what you feel, what you think.

What's stirring in you today, in this moment? Did anything from the reading in this section capture your heart's or mind's attention?

How does this idea of the vital tribe strike you? Have you experienced an interconnected weaving of the Sacred, trusted soul friends, and your expansive human family? Does that call to you, draw you in anew or for the first time? Does one of the strands intrigue or turn you off more than the others?

What has been your experience with self-help and personal transformation? Has it been isolated or communal? Has it been empowering and valuable? How does the idea of a journey of deep transformation in the context of a *kula*, a community of the heart, strike you?

Have you had an experience of coming alive while listening to or talking with someone about what is important and what really matters to you? If you haven't, begin imagining what that would be like, with whom that conversation might occur, and what you might talk about.

Engage (commit)

A nudge. Talk to someone you trust about your experience with a deeply relational experience of the Sacred, with soul friends, with your larger human family. Speak about what has been easy and hard, healing and hurting, in the midst of this vital tribe.

Now, it's your turn. What or who are you beckoned to *commit to, connect with*, or *create*—whether in small or big ways?

Share something from this PoP with someone you trust.

Your Word. Write a word that has captured your attention in this PoP.

BE BOLD. BE BRAVE. BE YOU.

Surrounded by Sacred

THERE ARE MANY WAYS TO CONNECT WITH THE SACRED ...
THAT SOMETHING OR SOMEONE GREATER THAN YOU.

It's stunning to see the diverse ways in which people cultivate this part of themselves—within and outside of religious communities; in buildings of worship and outside in nature; practicing yoga, prayer, and meditation; and on and on.

My friend, in order to be transparent, so that you know exactly where I am in terms of the Sacred, here is what is true for me, in a raw and real, nothin'-to-hide sort of a way. God is the warp and woof of me and has always been my heartbeat, my Tour Guide in life—whether in moments of pain or joy, in times of knowing or uncertainty, when feeling like a rock star or at rock bottom. God is the ultimate Source of everything good in my life. The starting point for my connection with God is Jesus. This has been true for me ever since I was a little girl. I converse with Jesus, my ever-present brother, as I go about my days, hearing His voice speaking whatever I most need to hear every single time I listen.

My words for the Sacred are most often God and Jesus. Thus, when I speak of my personal life, I will use these words, my "first language" in my spiritual journey. But when it is about a collective spiritual journey, I will use the words Sacred and Spirit.

By virtue of the diversity in our human experience, I understand that these words or even the capitalization of the words will not work for everyone. In order to personalize the Sacred for yourself, freely substitute the words I use with the word or phrase that takes you most deeply into your spiritual connection. This, I hope, will keep us walking, growing, and *jOURneying* together in the days to come.

We have golden opportunities throughout much of life to learn from and listen to the varied ways others foster their spiritual journeys. Transparency about what matters to each of us, and being open to the same in others, can create magnificent bridges of connection. These bridges are particularly paramount in places of division—whether within our intimate relationships or in our local neighborhoods or distant countries.

The time is now
to create a community
with arms flung open
to each other,
in places of similarity and difference,
whether we share the same language or not.

Transparency about what matters to each of us, and being open to the same in others, can create magnificent bridges of connection.

Be Still (surrender)

I wonder,
what do you most need in your heart,
in your body, in your soul at this moment?
You don't need to know what it is.
You may just feel an ache,
or be worn out,
or happily content to sit down for a moment.

If there are a flurry of thoughts,
let them flurry off.
Bid them farewell for now.
Here, you just get to be.
Be and breathe.
Stay here for a few moments longer.

ponder (go deeper)

Listen to the song, "Dreams on Fire," from the movie *Slumdog Millionaire*, by A.R. Rahman, called the "Mozart of Madras." This piece speaks of belonging, love, passion, seeing, magic. Write about the words, the beauty, the true that calls to your heart here. Or listen to "Latika's Theme," also by A.R. Rahman. This is a variation of the song "Dreams on Fire." I chose this song with the intention that the absence of words in this musical piece will open up the space for the "song that is your life" to become more clear, more compelling, and more graced than ever. May these songs gently, yet unmistakably, open your heart, your soul, your very self, to a bit more of your glittering worth and your one-of-a-kind purpose on the planet. Go for a walk with the song as your companion.

How important has your spiritual journey been to you, as you have navigated through life until now? What dreams and desires do you have around connecting with, opening to, and dialoguing with the Sacred in the midst of your life today, in this very moment?

How might you, your community, and our world be different if we did not reject *other* faith communities? How comfortable are you sitting with and listening to those with different spiritual beliefs than you? Do you try to change them and attempt to make them understand your way? Or, do you hide your spiritual beliefs or big parts of yourself in fear that others will reject you if they see this part of you?

Many have had challenging experiences with religion or the ways human beings have distorted religion. Have you? If so, ponder and write about your story. Has it been a source of division within you and your personal connection with the Sacred? Has it separated you from others who are part of a religious tradition you have struggled with?

Engage (commit)

A nudge. This week, reach out with curiosity, in your unique way, to someone of a different faith. Have a conversation. Ask questions and listen.

Now, it's your turn. What or who are you beckoned to *commit to, connect with,* or *create*—whether in small or big ways?

Share something from this PoP with someone you trust.

Your Word. Write a word that has captured your attention in this PoP.

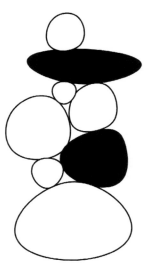

BE BOLD. BE BRAVE. BE YOU.

Trusted Soul Friends

FOR ME, THERE IS NO DOUBT, NOT ONE SINGLE DOUBT, THAT I COULD NOT HAVE DONE MUCH OF ANYTHING ON MY LIFE'S JOURNEY WITHOUT MY TRUSTED SOUL FRIENDS.

They spur me to keep going every single day. There have been many times I would have been trapped in the muck and mire of fear, hurt, or discouragement without these trusted soul friends.

You, too, need a trusted few with whom you can be you—to laugh or cry, to rock life or flail, to be loud or be quiet. These are the ones with whom you are able to be real, together. Living a life of raw and real interconnection makes life better.

The stories that are in us to live, we cannot write into existence alone. It may seem more comfortable to *learn* lessons and be vulnerable in private … say, in the pages of our journals or in quiet times of contemplation and prayer. Although times of solitude have riches of their own, there is an essential element of expansive growth that is *kindled in the company of others.* We need others to *reflect* back to us what they see, to *beckon* us to places we cannot reach alone, to *listen* to what matters to us, to *witness* our bold (albeit trembling) moments of voicing our stories.

Enter deeper still
into the mystery
that the capacity and provision
of a *kula*
is breathtaking and game-changing.

It is here where
you discover and uncover
the powerful and propelling ways in which
we are inextricably
tied together.

You, too, need a trusted few with whom you can be you—to laugh or cry, to rock life or flail, to be loud or be quiet. These are the ones with whom you are able to be real, together. Living a life of raw and real interconnection makes life better.

It is here where
you are beckoned and empowered
to be bold,
to be brave,
to be you.

I am convinced that
we cannot be fully
human if we are
not part of
community where
we belong.
-Kathleen Fay
kula sister

Be Still (surrender)

In the midst of the reality or dream
of a *kula* of trusted soul friends in your life,
this is a moment of sacred solitude.
Yes, shhhhh.
Breathe. Be still.
Tend to being.
Being still.
Not doing one single thing.
Just be.
Right here, right now.

ponder (go deeper)

Listen to "Brighter Than the Sun," sung by Colbie Caillat. Feel the glow of your life, of those around you, of this very day. Bask in the words of connection, of love, of being kindled by one another, as in a mighty flash of lightening. Write about what words, what parts capture your heart.

What's percolating in you? Is it something related to these stories or this content or is it something totally separate from what you've read thus far? Whatever is beginning to bubble up, write on that, sit with that, be with that. Your story is unfolding in its own way and time, with unique-to-you content.

What is your sense of *kula*, a community of trusted soul friends, in your life currently? Is there no one, or is there one individual, or many with whom you can be real and raw? Do you have any little or big hopes around what your tribe looks and feels like in your life?

Engage (commit)

A nudge. In our family and with my friends, we often speak of sharing a rose (something exciting and growing), a bud (something you're looking forward to), and a thorn (something difficult). Find someone today to share your rose, bud, and thorn with and ask them to share the same.

Now, it's your turn. What or who are you beckoned to *commit to*, *connect with*, or *create*—whether in small or big ways?

Share something from this PoP with someone you trust.

Your Word. Write a word that has captured your attention in this PoP.

BE BOLD. BE BRAVE. BE YOU.

Shared Humanity

ENLARGING YOUR VISION FOR AND COMMITMENT TO THOSE "STRANGERS" IN YOUR COLOSSAL AND COMMON HUMAN FAMILY CHANGES YOUR THOUGHTS, ACTIONS, AND HEART … SOMETIMES IN EVERYDAY AND SMALL WAYS AND AT OTHER TIMES IN LIFE-ALTERING EPIC WAYS.

It is here that a sense of belonging to, *comPASSIONate* attention to, and responsibility for one another grows—whether with those unknown or known to you.

How might it alter our engagement with people portrayed in the news and on social media if we saw them not as *strangers* but as people connected to us? Might it result in lessening judgment, fear, and distrust? I have a hunch the answer is yes. It has been in my life. And I see it happening all over the world in both little and large ways.

Imagine the mighty movement
that would be unleashed if,
one by one,
we each opened up our minds and hearts
to those we don't yet know, love, or call friend or family.
We would see anew.
We would see these strangers as our own.
We would care about what matters to them.

This simple and humble opening shifts
what we think, talk about, and choose to do.
It changes everything.
It changes us.

How might it alter our engagement with people portrayed in the news and on social media if we saw them not as strangers but as people connected to us?

Be Still (surrender)

Whew.
These notions are big and important.
Big, yes.
Important, heck yeah.
But for now,
your big act is to breathe, to be still, to be silent.
To slow and surrender.
Be.
Breathe.

Whether for ten seconds or ten minutes.
Stay here, being and breathing.

ponder (go deeper)

Listen to the themes of sticking together in hope and faith in this powerful song, "One Day," sung by Matisyahu. It's on my daily playlist. Every time I listen to it, there is a sonic boom in my heart.

Pick one phrase or idea from this section and look, listen, learn. Write about or head out for a walk and consider the parts in the message that beckon your attention.

Do you have a sense or an experience of being interconnected with others—all others—in the world? Does that excite or scare you, draw you in or repel you?

Engage (commit)

A nudge. Look for one time today to act with more grace and love with a stranger or friend in the midst of the raw and real of life (errands, work, family, email … anything that captures your attention), because of this deep and real interconnection. A few vignettes of ideas of how this might look …

You are cut off in traffic or in the grocery line, and out of a keep-it-real commitment to do your little part in the moment, you respond to that person in a way tinged with love. Respond as you would to a person very dear to you.

On your next drive or walk, whatever are the paths and parts of your life where you bump up against strangers, you say hello and smile as you pass people, perhaps sharing a private prayer or blessing in your own way.

You see social media as a meaningful microphone with which you get to share a message of love, friendship, and encouragement with friends near and far. Or, you choose to unplug for an hour, a day, or a week from digital media in order to make space to connect with people right next to you.

At your next social gathering, you mix up the conversation and talk about things that really matter, that excite, perplex, challenge, and intrigue you. You share your tiny or supersized dream. You ask what's really going on in the lives of those at the gathering.

Now, it's your turn. What or who are you beckoned to *commit to*, *connect with*, or *create*—whether in small or big ways?

Share something from this PoP with someone you trust.

Your Word. Write a word that has captured your attention in this PoP.

BE BOLD. BE BRAVE. BE YOU.

Arms Flung Open

HAVE YOU BEEN TEMPTED TO LOP OFF LIMBS OR HIDE BIG PARTS OF YOURSELF, BELIEVING THAT IF YOU SHARE *THAT* ASPECT OF WHO YOU ARE, PEOPLE WILL BE UNABLE TO HANDLE IT AND WILL TURN AWAY?

Have you lived scared that you will be misunderstood and judged if you truthfully speak about *that thing*? Take a look at the diversity that exists between you and those *nearest and dearest* to you: your spouse, kids, family, or closest friends.

Begin to *explore, experiment with, and experience* what happens when you walk more often open to those who seem uncomfortably *unlike* you. Living with your *arms flung open* bridges *you with others*. This is a radical resolution, a brave way, to be sure. This is a courageous commitment that is even more important—and perhaps difficult—when the dissimilarities are vast.

So my friend, how about it?
Are you ready to commit to living a bit more with
your arms flung open to yourself and to others?

When you do, you will discover and offer
a balm for healing,
energy for next steps and leaps,
joy for the arduous days,
meaning in the minutiae,
worth in the diminishment.

Begin to explore, experiment with, and experience what happens when you walk more often open to those who seem uncomfortably unlike you.

As you do,
you will find
kindred soldiers for the battle,
conceivers of
and
collaborators for your big dreams.

You—we—will be lit up
and
live ablaze.

Be Still (surrender)

My friend, take this time,
whether it's ten seconds or ten minutes.
Be here.
Be open.
Be still.

ponder (go deeper)

Listen to this rousing song by Imagine Dragons, "On Top of the World." *Ponder* and write about the words or phrases you love and the rhythms that get your toes tappin'.

What parts of yourself do you hide, fearing judgment or disconnection from people closest to you? Are they related to your political views, spiritual beliefs, the highs or lows of your bank account … or to how you look, how you feel, or something else?

Consider and/or write about two different experiences. One in which you shared yourself with another and it resulted in exclusion or separation, and one in which there was a profound exchange and a palpable sense of coming together. What elements do you see that set up the different outcomes? Be descriptive about the where, who, when, and how of it.

How might you invite others to be more real and raw, wholeheartedly sharing themselves with you? In what ways might this shift the ways in which you think about differences in the bigger community of your mighty human family?

Engage (commit)

A nudge. Find one time today to either share a raw and real part of yourself with another—a part you typically hide from others—and/or welcome the same in another. Consider having this interaction with someone near and dear to you, someone with whom you are very intimate, but from whom you hide a part of yourself.

Now, it's your turn. What or who are you beckoned to *commit to, connect with,* or *create*—whether in small or big ways?

Share something from this PoP with someone you trust.

Your Word. Write a word that has captured your attention in this PoP.

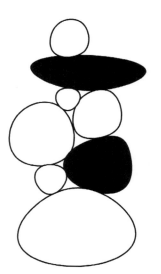

BE BOLD. BE BRAVE. BE YOU.

practices & perspectives

This *jOURney* is a simple one
of sharing and exchanging a few seeds of stories,
watching for tendrils of what grows in you
and working it into the soil of your everyday life.

The practices and perspectives that follow
will kindle, awaken, and illuminate
more of what matters most to you,
lighting you up with a clearer vision than ever
for your purpose on the planet.

Who knows, maybe this excitement
will be felt by those closest to you
or begin to take shape to connect
with the lives of those
in far-flung neighborhoods in the world.

Simple & Small

THE SMALL AND SIMPLE CAN INDEED BE SIGNIFICANT. THEY CAN BE MORE THAN ENOUGH.

This *jOURney* is not necessarily about making big changes. It is about humbly committing to the value of doing small things, of reaching out to others with great love.

One of my dear soul friends, Raquel, is a momma of triplet boys who are two years old and to a little girl who is five. Life is, shall we say, *full*. In the midst of the daily work of caring for her brood of little ones, she has created a sanctuary by surrounding her young tribe with music, feasting, books, prayer, and laughter.

Raquel is fiercely committed to intentionally planting seeds of kindness, beauty, faith, and joy in her children, each and every day. To that end, Raquel asks her children to do an act of love for their family each day *that goes unnoticed*. Raquel beckons her little ones to practice quietly simple acts of kindness. It is woven into the everyday … *humbly performed without fanfare*.

My goodness. Can you imagine if we each took on Raquel's invitation and committed to offering one daily act of love that goes unnoticed? Quietly simple service like this could light up the world.

Sometimes we may see the ripples
of these little, often-invisible acts,
and at other times, we won't.
Perhaps this is one of the gifts
of these humble *DOings*:
to be free from the need to know
where they will lead,
but to simply serve.
To be love.

Small things with great, great love. This is compassion. Compassion is not pity. Pity is your pain in my heart. It just sits there. It heals nothing. But compassion. Compassion is your pain in my heart and back out through my hands.
-Glennon Doyle Melton, Momastery blog

Be Still (surrender)

Close your eyes.
Relax your brow, your jaw.
Take five deep, long, breaths.
Exhale audibly,
as if releasing a loud sigh,
letting go of whatever worries, burdens, or conundrums you carry.

Stay here for as many seconds or minutes as you are able.

Ponder (go deeper)

Listen to "One Love," sung by Playing for Change. What pops up in your mind and heart as you do? Something in the music, the lyrics? Find and watch the video and if you are so inspired, look into the goodness this music and community have unleashed.

What strikes you in this chapter about the simple, about small acts done with great love? Does anything come to mind that connects to your own life?

What is something you can do that may feel small, but that you can begin today in service to those near or far? Elevate this small thing in your thinking. Commit to it with conviction. Trust. Listen. Look around. You will get an answer, a nudge for the ways in which that small thing might become something wondrous. Beware of the subtle and diminishing judgment that may try to stop you by suggesting that what you do must be big to be important. Sometimes, it's the smallest, most imperceptible thoughts and actions that invoke the mightiest change.

Engage (commit)

A nudge. Today, do one act of love that goes unnoticed. *Bonus nudge #1:* Write about how it feels. Do you want to do it more? Did you find it easy or hard? *Bonus nudge #2:* Keep going and do one daily act of love that goes unnoticed for one week.

Now, it's your turn. What or who are you beckoned to *commit to, connect with,* or *create*—whether in small or big ways?

Share something from this PoP with someone you trust.

Your Word. Write a word that has captured your attention in this PoP.

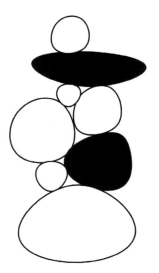

BE BOLD. BE BRAVE. BE YOU.

Ebbing & Flowing

TOO MUCH OF EITHER OF THESE MOVEMENTS IS UNBALANCED AND UNSUSTAINABLE. IT SETS THE STAGE FOR DISASTER.

Neither the ocean nor you can function for long without the regular, rhythmic patterns of *both* ebb and flow, quiet and action, solitude and community, self-care and service.

Ebb living for too long can become a place of hiding, withdrawing, and isolation. It can make for too many low-energy days. You were meant for more. You were meant to *do*, to *flow*, energized by expressing your unique purpose on the planet. So, if you find yourself in never-ending ebb living, it may be time to kindle and spark those dreams, say yes more often, and spread your arms a bit wider.

Conversely, continuous flow living can find you exhausted and overwhelmed in the unending pressure to do more and the relentless push to power forward. You may find yourself in the grueling surge of never-ending work and incessant to-do lists. *Oof*. It may be time to cultivate a rhythm of *bistari* (that beautiful Nepali word for "slowly"), of intentional and regular pauses. To be still. To be quiet. To rest.

This intentional and rhythmic movement of ebb and flow living will change you. Your senses will be tuned to when you need to re-center by moving more towards one or the other.

Your fuel tank will be on empty less often.
You will dream big and love bigger.
More often, your arms will be
merrily flung open to your human family.
Your vision will be expanded
to embrace a life of inspired doing
and the nourishing stillness of being.

A silent heart is a loving heart, and a loving heart is a hospice to the world ... My life of service and love to my fellow man is simply the echo of this silence and solitude ... Now I become as one on fire with love of Him and all humanity.
-Catherine Doherty
Poustinia

Be Still (surrender)

Right here, right now, breathe.
Inhale deeply, fully. Exhale deeply, fully.
Close your eyes, soften your jaw, your eyebrows, and breathe.

Do some gentle neck circles. Listen, look within.
If there are places in your body where you're feeling tight, let go of worry.
Just notice.
Imagine softening your furrowed brow, constricted stomach, or tight jaw.
For at least three full breath cycles, close your eyes and breathe.

Here and now. Trust, just trust. Do less. Try less. Push less.
Be open. Let go.
Be.

ponder (go deeper)

Listen to (and watch the video, if you can) "Follow the Sun," sung by Xavier Rudd. Bask in the poetry, the invitation of this song, to breathe, dream, set intentions, cherish, and let go. *Ahh.*

Do you feel that you have been ebbing for too long? Do you retreat, pull back, or recede too often? Write about a time in which you imagine yourself bravely and committedly living into more of the flow that's calling to you. Or, recall a time that such a golden moment occurred. What are/were you doing? Where are/were you? How does/did it feel? What would excite you to explore and move into some of this surging forward momentum?

Do you need more *bistari*, more rest or stillness? To *slow down* just a bit? Do you believe that the more you do, the more value, success, worth you have? This can be an exhaustive loop. Have you been surging forward, working without pause for too long? Expand and explore these ideas while on a walk or in your journal.

Ask for a whisper of something you need to hear right now from within you or from Spirit. Listen and allow the answers to come through. You will hear and know.

Engage (commit)

A nudge. Dream and create a few things that will make space for what you most need right now. A few ideas: What about a morning, an evening, or a day each week of regular rest—some faith traditions call this Sabbath. In my life, I've made a new commitment to take one weekday a month to not work. For me, this takes great courage, surrender, and radical *trust*.

Now, it's your turn. What or who are you beckoned to *commit to, connect with,* or *create*—whether in small or big ways?

Share something from this PoP with someone you trust.

Your Word. Write a word that has captured your attention in this PoP.

BE BOLD. BE BRAVE. BE YOU.

Garden Life

LIVING IN COLORADO, THERE ARE FOUR DISTINCTIVELY DIFFERENT SEASONS. EACH ONE BRINGS DIFFERENCES IN TEMPERATURE AND CLIMATE, AS WELL AS CHANGES IN THE APPEARANCE AND PACE OF NATURE.

One recent summer day, my garden spoke to me. Deeply. It beckoned me to come and see, to *be still* and *ponder*.

As I did, I saw it clearly. There was far too much growing too close together. At this rate, the plants would start to choke out each other and no longer be able to thrive. The garden needed to be thinned in order to allow each plant ample room—without having to compete with other plants.

The same is true for us. At times, there is a need for attentive space-making to cultivate conditions for vibrant growth, while at other times we must trust that the starkness around us is necessary and temporary. A garden and nature's seasons remind us that life and growth are happening no matter what things may look like outwardly, with each season offering distinct ways to move through our days.

Wherever you are in the season of life,
may your time of seeding,
lying dormant,
maturing,
producing,
harvesting,
exchanging,
and flourishing
be blessed.

Above all, trust in the slow work of God. We are quite naturally impatient in everything to reach the end without delay. We should like to skip the intermediate stages. We are impatient of being on the way to something unknown, something new.
- Teilhard de Chardin excerpt of prayer-poem, "Patient Trust"

Be Still (surrender)

No matter the season in your life's garden,
pause here.
Be here.
Breathe here.
Let the thoughts that come
be gently plucked from your thinking mind.
Let the worries be weeded.
Bask in the soil of this space, this place of rest.
You are loved.
BEloved.
Breathe it in.
And let everything else go.

ponder (go deeper)

Listen to "Amazing Day," sung by Coldplay. Take in the invitation. What can you cultivate to foster hope, wonder, beauty, a place to *be who you are* and cultivate what you
need most on this amazing day?

Imagine your life and yourself as a plant. What do you see, sense? How are your roots?
How is the soil around you? Do you need some nutrients, more light, more water? What
surrounds you? What other plants grow nearby? What is your environment like? Does a
transplant to another environment beckon?

What season are you in right now? Have you been dormant long enough and now feel
ready for a season of spring or summer, to burst into growth and bloom? What do you

need? More nutrients, some thinning, some expert gardeners? Some *stakes* of support—of daily rhythms or a trusted tribe?

Have you been growing too fast for too long and do you long for a time of dormancy—for some dark, quiet, and reflective space? If you find yourself hungering for a season of fall or winter, it might be wise for you to support the slower and quieter rhythms of life. Is this a time to hold off on those big ideas and plans, choosing to let them sit, maybe to go underground for now?

If so, explore ways that you can benefit from going in, going deep, getting still. Be inspired by the reminder from nature that bulb plants need seasons of cool, quiet darkness, underground, to be prepared for the day they pop above the soil, their stunning blossoms signaling that a new day has come.

Engage (commit)

A nudge. Choose one thing to *do today* that will respond to what the garden of your life most needs: nourishment, support, creating, or space for the season in which you find yourself now.

Now, it's your turn. What or who are you beckoned to *commit to*, *connect with*, or *create*—whether in small or big ways?

Share something from this PoP with someone you trust.

Your Word. Write a word that has captured your attention in this PoP.

BE BOLD. BE BRAVE. BE YOU.

Letting Go & Wading In

I'VE DISCOVERED I CAN LOVE AND SERVE MOST WHOLEHEARTEDLY AND DEEPLY WHEN I RELEASE ANY SENSE THAT FIXING THE PROBLEM IS ENTIRELY UP TO ME.

Most often, the solution is beyond me. That's the truth 99.9% of the time.

This *letting go* is humbling and freeing. And, I've come to see that *letting go* is often accompanied by a nudge to *wade in*. This is another one of those complementary both/ands of soulful living. These opposites are often connected. Watch for it in the days to come.

Wading in is about compassionately getting close to one who is struggling—seeing, listening, and *being with* them. It most often involves a time to *be still* and *ponder*, "What is my part, if any?" It may be followed by a palpable sense that it is time for me to *participate* and *do* something, but to do so free of the sense that it's my job to fix the person or the problem. Again: most everything is greater than my capacity to solve.

I have also come to know that in order to *wade in* and be with people throughout the sorrows of life, I must develop a regular, rhythmic practice of humbly letting go. I believe, with all my heart, that the same is true for you. Whether the one you love is a toddler teething, a teenager individuating, a spouse isolating, a news story highlighting the broken and terrifying, *let go* … and *wade in*.

Letting go frees.
It humbles.
It is peaceful.
It is an exhale.

> Letting go beckons. It calls us to wade in and tend to those we are destined to serve and *enCOURAGES* us to light up the world with our purpose on the planet.

It buffers us from the illusion
that we can or ought to try to save the world
and
protects us from being burned out
by the burden of overzealousness.

Letting go beckons.
It calls us to wade in and
tend to those we are destined to serve
and *enCOURAGES* us
to light up the world
with our purpose on the planet.

Be Still (surrender)

Right here, right now,
shhhhhh.
Don't worry, contemplate, or think.
Soften your gaze, your jaw, your brow.
Breathe—long and deep.
Exhale—long and deep.
Close your eyes.
Stay here for a bit.

ponder (go deeper)

Listen to "One Step Closer to You," sung by Michael Franti and Spearhead. Allow the invitation to let go pulse within you, flow over you, quiet you. And, if you feel like it, be free and hop up to dance and move a bit.

Think about a persistent worry or place of anxiety in your life. What do you think about as you drive down the road that makes your jaw tight and your head ache? Right here, right now, before the problem or challenge that captures your attention is resolved, pause. Release the burden to fix this, if only for a moment.

Cup your hands. Look at the bowl of your cupped hands. Imagine the person or the problem that burdens you resting in your hands. Invite the Sacred to come in, to be there, with that person or problem, in your cupped hands. Or ask the Sacred to scoop this problem or person up and out of your hands with infinite care and love, caring for all of it with infinite capacity and love. Do you feel a lift, a lessening of the burden? Stay here and really imagine it, with as many details as you can.

How would *letting go* and *wading in* impact your everyday life, those nearest and dearest to you? How might this shift the way you spend time with your kids, or nudge you to head out on a date with your loved one, spend an evening sitting and talking with friends till late into the evening, or watch a movie that expands your imagination and awareness of something that matters to you?

Engage (commit)

A nudge. Let go of any pressure to fix the person or solve the problem and then *wade in and be* with a person who is struggling. Just be there. Listen. Connect. Witness.

Now, it's your turn. What or who are you beckoned to *commit to, connect with,* or *create*—whether in small or big ways?

Share something from this PoP with someone you trust.

Your Word. Write a word that has captured your attention in this PoP.

BE BOLD. BE BRAVE. BE YOU.

Robust Rhythms

GRATITUDE IS ONE OF THE MOST SUSTAINABLE AND SIMPLE WAYS TO RECHARGE AND STAY CHARGED.

Maybe you're thinking, *Yeah, yeah, grateFULLness is important. I know it is. But, right now, life is hard ... too hard.* I feel you. I've been there, too. *Oof.* To be sure, there may be much that clamors for you to live in fear, fatigue, and scarcity.

Your current reality may be that you feel bone-tired and desperately low on bandwidth, with no place to rest in sight. Life can seem heavy and hard when fear and anxiety about what hasn't yet happened, what you still don't have, and what is wrong preoccupy your mind. Consider for a moment what recent research in the field of neuroscience has shown us: whatever we focus on gets bigger. It grows.

This is where gratitude and looking for the good comes in. It's one of those simple, but not easy, practices. In the midst of life here and now—particularly in the hard, the painful, and the challenging—when you cultivate the habit of looking for the good, when you practice thankfulness in more bits of life, when you *really* remember it, you change.

> When your heart fills up and gets more jam-packed with *grateFULLness*, you begin to see the vastness, the plenty, and the abundance of gifts within your life and in the world around you.

The funk and difficulties may not be gone, but you are different and the world seems different. When your heart fills up and gets more jam-packed with *grateFULLness*, you begin to see the vast- ness, the plenty, and the abundance of gifts within your life and in the world around you. The mishaps and mistakes morph into building blocks of hope and the not-knowing doesn't stop you from walking with your head held high and your eyes sparkling. The days shift to being fueled by your unstoppable purpose rather than by lack and overwhelm—from the time you rise until the time you fall into bed at night. Sounds pretty good, aye?

Let's take a moment to explore your day, one part at a time, weaving in PoPs—practices, perspectives, and *gratefulness*—to keep your battery charged and your focus where it will best serve you.

Morning. What simple rituals or practices can you envision creating that would provide a morning experience filled with joy? How might they prevent you from being derailed by thoughts tinged with worry, overwhelm, or the unknown, allowing you to look right at them and respond with ease? What would cause you to increase the level of eagerness—a little or a lot—with which you greet your day? Is it sipping a cozy drink, sitting in a certain place, going for a walk or a run, reading, meditating, writing, or creating a bit more time for getting ready?

Midday. Is there a five-minute midday opportunity each day when you might consider the *good* that's happened in the morning, and pause, breathe, and go outside? On the warm days, might you take a walk, feeling the sun warming your skin or the cool breeze touching you? On days that are too chilly or too wet to head outside, could you sit at a window and look out at nature with a steaming cup of tea?

Evening. How might you end your day each night—is there anything you might shift that would fuel and sustain you with a bit more feel-good juju as you look back at your day and forward to the day ahead? Is it getting to bed earlier, sitting with your partner over a delicious evening drink, taking a bath, reading an inspirational book, or listening to a piece of music that swells your heart?

You need these rhythms and ways of *DOing* and *BEing* as surely as you need air to breathe.

May your eyes see ripples
of beauty and possibility all around you,
here and now.

May you know the things
to which to say yes and no,
making plentiful space
for a life that blossoms beyond
your biggest dreams and greatest fears.

May courage and conviction
eclipse anxiety for your next steps and leaps.

May your vision be deeply rooted
and grow expansively beyond
what you ever thought possible.

May you live bold and brave among your tribe
of your mighty human family and the Sacred.

May your heart be both soft and fierce,
fueling you to hope and love big.

Be Still (surrender)

Take this moment,
whatever time of day it is,
wherever you find yourself,
and just be.
This is not the time to do, think, plan, consider.
Breathe.
Relax.
Stay here, for a few or many minutes.

ponder (go deeper)

Listen to "Perfect Timing (This Morning)" by Orba Squara. Imagine some of the elements of your perfect morning stretching into your day and evening. Write about it or walk and *ponder* it.

How are your daily PoPs feeling and working? Are you settling into a rhythm that feels good to you? If not, write a bit about deepening your practice and commitment to a daily PoP. Get detailed about it: time of day, length of PoP, place, other elements—including a cozy drink, books, journal.

What might be ways for you to take a pause midday or end your day that will feel good, fuel you, and bring renewed strength and vitality into your life? Try them. See which ones you like most, and commit to regularly cultivating them in your life.

Do you feel the *low battery* warning go off regularly? What can you imagine implementing as portable charging stations for the road—to fuel you up during the day as needed? How do you *charge up* yourself for the daily rigors that are bound to occur? Are there practices you notice other people doing that would be fun to try when responding to stress in the moment or low energy during your day?

Keep in mind that a spontaneous, spur-of-the-moment PoP can be a powerful way to respond when life hits you with a stressful trigger. Taking some time to pause, ponder, and consider what you want to do to engage with the challenge from a place of wisdom, truth, voice, courage, and love can lead to intentional actions rather than knee-jerk reactions.

Would your heart and life be buoyed a bit by gratitude? Write about what would shift. Explore if there are any specific places or relationships in which you'd like to commit to being more *grateFULL*. If you have a moment, check out GoodGoodGood.co online. It is all about cultivating the good through celebrating and becoming accomplices in good work. Their print *Goodnewspaper* and online e-newsletter, the *Goodnewsletter*, are stunning examples of looking for the good. How about creating your own daily *Goodnewsletter* and writing one gratitude each day in a journal, on your bathroom mirror, or via a text to yourself?

Engage (commit)

A nudge. Commit to a pocket of time today to *be* in silence, when there is typically noise and conversation. Try it. Turn off the radio, your TV, maybe even play with having a meal in silence with those in your life … explore what bubbles up. If you like it, do it again tomorrow.

Now, it's your turn. What or who are you beckoned to *commit to, connect with*, or *create*—whether in small or big ways?

Share something from this PoP with someone you trust.

Your Word. Write a word that has captured your attention in this PoP.

BE BOLD. BE BRAVE. BE YOU.

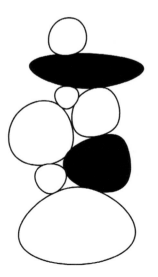

2

[flickering]

shining with a wavering light. burning
irregularly or unsteadily.

It's time to move with *bistari*, slowing the pace greatly.
We will gently tend to the places of struggle—
whether in your life, in the life of one you love, or in the world around you.

As you do,
this is a bold claim and promise,
but an assured one:
beauty will emerge out of the ashes,
eyes dulled with loss and grief will sparkle with joy,
wrists once shackled will rise and fall in grateful dancing,
voices that were once diminished will now shout with courageous conviction,
moments rippling with possibility will replace dead-end days,
strength will be forged in the midst of struggle.

In the many diverse places we find ourselves,
particularly the deeply challenging ones,
take heart and know that the struggle will not last forever.
Sometimes hope is particularly hard to see, but it is there.

The fear, darkness, and struggles
that are in the world or within you may be massive,
but they are trumped by love and light and hope—always.

Courageously tend to these broken-hearted places.
A light is flickering.
If the flicker seems extremely low, take heart.
Remember, the darker the place, the more a light glows.
Hope is kindling and will burst out of the ashes.

when life is hard

If you are reading this
with a heart or body throbbing with pain,
I'm sending love to you, intending and praying
for you to feel seen, companioned, and supported.
The struggle need not be the end of your story.

Do you lament?
"I can't do this. I'm stuck."
"I can't imagine lighting UP the world."
"There is way too much that's broken in my own life."
If so, you're not alone.

There can be pain—great oceans of it—
in us, around us.
Allow what is broken in you or in the world
to capture your attention.
Pause and tend to these places.
You will find surprises and treasures here—
in these deep chasms lie gemstones.

Out of the darkest places,
the pain that cripples and blinds, right here,
there is love, hope, and healing.

Struggling

BEING HUMAN CAN BE HARD.

Bugger moments of heartbreak arise in and around you all the time.

Maybe life has been clipping along at a satisfactory—or spectacular—rate, but you are aware of pain in the life of someone you love or in the lives of those in far-off places. Or perhaps it's been a really tough week, month, and year for you … a too-long-stretch of hard days filled with confusion and overwhelm. The everyday human strains of health, finances, relationships, or work may have fallen heavy and hard in your lap.

A nudge. Don't run way. Stay here. The goodness to be discovered often lies among the hard, the dark, and the brutal. Although struggle need not have the last word in your story, there is a step you must take before getting to the joy, freedom, and healing.

You must acknowledge. You must see. You must look. At what has hurt. At what terrifies. At what is hard. In the world around you. In the lives of those you love. Within you.

Yes, you. Herein lies the root of your story. This story is your very own. There is a great gift in owning and embracing the whole of your story. However you see or feel about it, even if it seems ordinary, insufficient, meaningless, too broken, or not enough in some way, I invite you to look at it. Dare I nudge you further? *Wrap your arms around* the good, the bad, and the ugly that has happened to you or to those you love in days past or maybe even today.

A nudge. Don't run way. Stay here. The goodness to be discovered often lies among the hard, the dark, and the brutal.

> The wound is the place where the Light enters you.
> -Rumi

Here, right here, relax.
Let go and trust that wherever you find yourself
—right here, right now—
is just the right place.

At this very moment, there are treasures to be found in the dirt,
in the hidden, in the deep, dark crevices,
in the real bits and pieces in and around you.
Your story is waiting to be written … and lived.

Be Still (surrender)

Oof. Pain.
Are you in it?
Or is someone you love in it?
Sending an ocean of love to you, right here, right now.

Whatever is burdening you, imagine tucking the biggies into a backpack.
Is it heavy? Whew—mine sure can be, too.
Imagine, for a moment, that you take off that heavy backpack and set it aside.
Yes, yes—there may be things in it you'll need to tend to later.
But for now, can you, one strap at a time, take it off, and put it down?

Breathe.
Be.

ponder (go deeper)

Listen to "Touch the Sky," sung by Hillsong United, which speaks to the gifts in letting go, reaching out in surrender, and being swept up in love.

Write about how you feel regarding your story now—what's working, what's not? What makes your knees tremble? What gives you butterflies? What excites, what terrifies? Where are the places of crushing pain and heartbreak in the lives of those around you or in the very real and epic tragedies in the world? Is there sorrow in you that leaves you feeling kicked in the gut?

Are there poems or texts in your spiritual tradition that are wise and deep—that encourage you, and remind you to not give up hope in times of mess and chaos, when the world seems upside down and inside out? If not, I share a beautiful passage from my daily sacred text, the Bible, about creation in a moment of chaos and darkness:

Earth was a soup of nothingness,
a bottomless emptiness, an inky blackness.
God's Spirit brooded like a bird above the watery abyss
and began to see, speak, and create beauty.

Write about the places you feel or see nothingness. Ask the Spirit to speak into this … watch for images or listen for words. See what comes. Get ready to be surprised.

Write about or walk and consider the pain within you, in the life of one dear to you, and in the world. How might you be propelled to share more of yourself or embrace more of others in that *flinging your arms open* way, to be different and act differently?

Engage (commit)

A nudge. Set up a text thread, a regular video call, or conference call to check in and promise to keep it raw and real with a soul friend or two. Use the power of technology to connect real time throughout the amazing and hard days of life.

Now, it's your turn. What or who are you beckoned to *commit to, connect with,* or *create*—whether in small or big ways?

Share something from this PoP with someone you trust.

Your Word. Write a word that has captured your attention in this PoP.

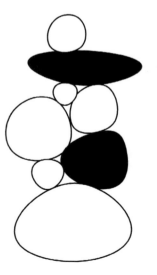

BE BOLD. BE BRAVE. BE YOU.

Messaging

IT IS TOO LATE.
I DO NOT MATTER.
I HAVE NOTHING TO OFFER.
I DO NOT HAVE WHAT I NEED.
I AM ALONE—ALWAYS HAVE BEEN, ALWAYS WILL BE.
THERE IS NO GOOD THAT CAN COME FROM THIS SITUATION.
BECAUSE I DID THIS (OR DIDN'T DO THAT), THERE IS NO HOPE.

When unseen and unacknowledged, diminishing messages and thoughts can crush you. They wage war. They pervasively dishearten, leaving you listless and dreamless.

But when you know the ones to which you are most vulnerable, you can be on the lookout for them and you can replace them with words that are *expansive* and *true*.

The power of the messages in this toxic self-talk is in their impact to lure you into believing that they will always be true and that hope is lost. When they are *tinged with truth*, they can loom even bigger. For instance, at times, you may indeed find yourself low on money, time, energy, or support. But, take heart. These small-minded messages are not ultimately true. Every last bit of your life, particularly the hard and hope-less bits, can be transformed into glittering gifts.

As you go about your day-to-day life, watch for the feelings of hopeless-ness that these messages often leave in their wake. When you have a decision to make or have a task to do, if you feel a lingering sense of discouragement, look for the feelings and motives behind these false messages and reach out for your tribe. Don't go it alone.

Every last bit of your life, particularly the hard and hopeless bits, can be transformed into glittering gifts.

Keep crafting the story of your life,
less influenced by these diminishing messages
and the applause of others.
You will live more free and less fettered than ever.
Keep walking and leaping,
with your head held high.
Keep dreaming,
with that gleam in your eye.

Be Still (surrender)

Silence the clamor of thoughts.
Thinking mind, be still.
Messages, pipe down.
Shhhhhh.
Breathe … deeply, fully, slowly.
With each breath, the pings of thoughts lessen.
With each breath, peace blankets your mind.

ponder (go deeper)

Do some battle, some dancing, some reframing of these messages as you rock out to "This is Me," sung by Keala Settle. Write about not being drowned out by words, not being ashamed, and living *boldly* ready to be *seen* and *heard*.

Flip one of your chronic small messages into its opposite. *I have nothing to offer* can be *My purpose is plentiful and my destiny great. I do not matter* can be *I have glittering worth.* Put this new commitment in a place where you will see it throughout the day. By doing so, you are doing battle and clearing a way for some new *delIGHT*.

Does your fear of what people think influence your day-to-day life? What would it feel like to be free of the burden to be always liked, understood, and affirmed by outside voices and to build a sense of worth and identity that is solid and secure in who you are? Where does that come from in your story?

I invite you to read aloud the following expansive messages and write down in your journal the ones that impact you:

I am loved—wildly, extravagantly, and wholly—because of who I AM.

I need not do one more thing to be more valuable.

I have a one-of-a-kind, never-seen-yet and never-to-be-seen-again purpose on the planet.

I will not measure or compare the value of my purpose, dreams, or destiny.

Engage (commit)

A nudge. Write down on little slips of paper the toxic messages and lies that you uncovered in your time of pondering above. Place them, one by one, before you. It may be a little pile of a few or a mountain of many. Scoop them up in your hands. Really be with them for a moment, here. Might you talk with the Sacred, One who loves you so wholly, about the letting go of these things? Then you choose: dump them into the trash bin, place them in your fireplace, or put them in fire-proof bowl and burn them. Watch them kindle and burn.

Now, it's your turn. What or who are you beckoned to *commit to, connect with,* or *create*—whether in small or big ways?

Share something from this PoP with someone you trust.

Your Word. Write a word that has captured your attention in this PoP.

BE BOLD. BE BRAVE. BE YOU.

Striving

OVER THE YEARS, I HAVE READ BOOKS BY MANY AN EXPERT TO UNCOVER MORE OF MY PALPABLE LIFE'S PURPOSE. I HAVE ENROLLED IN COURSES, GONE ON RETREATS, AND LIVED IN COMMUNITY. I HAVE WORKED AT IT. I HAVE *BECOME* MORE ME.

And yet, I see that I often stressed and strove in my becoming. I have often tried hard ... so hard ... too hard.

There have been seasons when I didn't know how to relax while on the *jOURney*, particularly in the midst of the unknown. There have been times when I put so much energy into figuring out my work, my destiny, and my part in the world that the joy of everyday living has been eclipsed.

The energy of striving and trying harder is exhausting and often does not lead to the places we are bound and determined to go. It may feel as if a light switch has flipped off and life becomes heavy and laborious.

There is a nuance, a subtlety to watch for here. Clues that the switch has gone off are when you feel that unrelenting energy of forcing and hard work ... a furrowed brow, grinding teeth, tight jaw, gut in pretzel knots, and sleepless nights. Here, you may feel it is all up to you, that there is not enough, that if you only did one more thing or tried just a bit harder, all would be well. This is an exhausting hamster wheel that never stops. There is no end to the striving, the measuring of your attempts, the visions for what more you might do in this crazy loop.

My friend, for you...
May there be
no more striving,
no more measuring
by

> You may feel it is all up to you, that there is not enough, that if you only did one more thing or tried just a bit harder, all would be well.

drip-drops
your contributions, your value, or your impact,
who you have been, are, or could be.

There are days coming that are bountiful and abundant,
that will overflow with fresh strength and power from within you,
such that you won't be able to catch or measure your dreams.

As you keep walking,
you will, step by step, become a bit more free...
and a lot more you.

Be Still (surrender)

Plop down.
Take a load off.
Relax.
Let go.
Stop.
Breathe.
Here and now, for as many moments as you can spare.

ponder (go deeper)

Listen to this beautyFULL song, "New Song," sung by Audrey Assad. She keeps it real and speaks of the feeling of coming undone, of the aches in life, and of the dream of a new song, a new way to speak and live. Close your eyes and listen … tend to the words, notes, and essence that speak to you.

What if the big dreams in you, the things you long for, or the path out of your current challenges, aren't about working more or trying harder? What if it's about *Pausing*, *Pondering*, and *Engaging* with curiosity and a bit of ease? Trust that you will see your next steps at just the right time.

If you find yourself low on inspiration and purpose in your daily acts of caring for family, or low in your joy quotient in work and high in overwhelm and discouragement, take these very real, human, everyday experiences and walk or write a bit about what you are feeling. Ask yourself if there is a new perspective or way to do this work. Consider if there is a trusted and wise person you can talk with about it all. How might it feel to bring these very things and open up your heart to the personal presence and power of the Sacred, who is here to support and propel you?

Engage (commit)

A nudge. Today, choose one time, one specific act, in which you typically work hard, too hard. But, today, you do not *try harder*. Ask for help in a daily arduous task or reach out to a person who can do with ease what is hard for you. Write about your observations in your journal or go for a walk with this experience.

Now, it's your turn. What or who are you beckoned to *commit to*, *connect with*, or *create*—whether in small or big ways?

Share something from this PoP with someone you trust.

Your Word. Write a word that has captured your attention in this PoP.

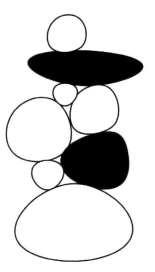

BE BOLD. BE BRAVE. BE YOU.

Starving

THERE WAS A DAY THAT MY HOPE DWINDLED TO A FLICKER, MY VOICE QUIETED TO A WHISPER, AND I ALMOST DIED.

The truth is, not many people know this part of my story. I've been reluctant to share it because I'm a little embarrassed. Almost two decades ago, I nearly starved myself to death in a land of plenty. I was lost and very, very alone. I doubted that I mattered.

The best I can tell from this vantage point, twenty-five years later, is that the roots of my eating disorder were strengthened by a few factors. They developed in unchecked, unrelenting, and untrue messages. They took over even more as I habitually looked for affirmation from others and tried harder. They were rooted in my flawed belief that my value and worth were connected to and elevated by my performance and success.

How I hope that you have never experienced this kind of dangerous addiction and rock-bottom doubt, loneliness, and fear. But perhaps my story sounds strikingly familiar to yours. Perhaps you have found your story in bits of mine. Whether the connection is from years past or where you are right now, shine a light, speak your truth, and get some support for what you need right here and now.

Fan the flame of your life … of your story.
When you do,
the darkness of the past
or even current challenges
are less scary and less palpable.
There is hope, my friend,
in speaking what is true,
in shining the light on these dark places,
and in claiming that this does not need to be the way
things always will be in your story.

Weak is the New Strong. Because there's nothing left to prove. God isn't playing the game so why would we? And grasping clinging earning comparing ranking is exhausting.
-Rob Bell

Be Still (surrender)

Take whatever is hard, whatever worries you carry,
whatever thoughts that are fluttering,
and exhale—big.

Imagine that you are breathing them out and away,
that you are inhaling
peace,
softness,
soul care, and
tender love.
Be held in tender love.
Stay here for a few moments.

ponder (go deeper)

In the midst of whatever noise is around you or within you, take another moment to
be. "Let's Be Still" sung by The Head and the Heart beckons. This is a lyric about the times
when things are torn down in order to rebuild. Reflect on times in your life when you have
felt this experience of dismantling, even if happening right now. Do you see any glimmers
of hope that have come out of those times? Write about this lyric-poetry and the feelings
that emerge, as you are quiet, here and now.

How do you speak to, think about, look at your body? What do you say to and about
your body? Do you drive it, force it, push it too hard? Do you objectify or judge its appear-
ance? Do you associate your value with how it does or doesn't look?

How might you open this up to the Spirit or your *kula* of trusted soul friends for some fresh messages and ways to think about your body in the days to come?

Is your body sick, tired, in pain, tight, or weak? Would it be helpful to have the support of a doctor, nutritionist, counselor, or support group to help you?

Do people or does the culture around you diminish or devalue you physically? Might you start a new conversation among those close to you about the value, dignity, and worth of our bodies? Do you need to increase your sense of power and security when it comes to your physical self … do you need others to support you in this? This is a challenge for our human family around the globe, to be sure. Regardless of where we live, how we live, or what we have or don't have, it can be a matter of life and death for many.

Engage (commit)

A nudge. Do one thing today to care for your body anew. Get more rest, move more or differently, drink more water, eat whole and healthy foods … maybe frolic and play a bit, just for the fun of it. Now, it's your turn. What or who are you beckoned to commit to, connect with, or create—whether in small or big ways?

Share something from this PoP with someone you trust.

Your Word. Write a word that has captured your attention in this PoP.

BE BOLD. BE BRAVE. BE YOU.

Wounding

WHEN I WAS AT THE PEAK OF MY EATING DISORDER, MY MIND, BODY, AND SOUL WERE SO DIS-EASED THAT THERE WAS LITTLE SOLACE IN TALKING TO OR BEING WITH OTHERS.

I remember those days, and they were gut-wrenching. Yet, in those days, more than ever, I needed people around me who lived with hope, a sense of vibrancy in their life, and who were dreaming big dreams. I needed their love and presence in my day-to-day life—it was one of the very things that kept me alive.

Are you walking wounded because of choices you've made that have encumbered or shackled you with addiction? If you stay alone in the pain, the regret, the shame, and the chaos of confusion, these wounds can leave you limping, hemorrhaging, and in the emergency room of life for many, many years—sometimes for an entire lifetime. There is another way. It need not be one of prolonged isolation, ache, or gripping pain.

Take heart, dear friend. There are times when words fail to communicate our deep places of hurt. If this moment finds you gripped by great pain and walking wounded, this is a time when I imagine us sitting together in my living room by the fire with a cup of steaming tea or slowly strolling together in that *bistari* way.

I hope this moment is imbued with some magic and that it touches you in a mysterious way. May whatever you most need slip into a crack in the doorway to your heart and fill you today. May you feel less alone. May you feel a flicker of hope, of a future, of love—perhaps a sense of anticipation for the days to come that you've not felt for a long time.

The word, *BEloved*, is one to sit with here and now. Soulfully consider if there is something to be discovered in living more loved than ever before. Might it hold solace for your soul, your body, your heart? If you are in a place of health and strength, might you enter into this next PoP with an intention to think about, send some good juju, or pray for someone you know who is currently in a place of pain and darkness?

May whatever you most need slip
into a crack in the doorway to your heart
and fill you today.
May you feel less alone.
May you sense from your core
your beautiful *BElovedness*
and flickers of
security and hope ... wholeness and strength
that buoys you this day.

When the words
stop
And you can endure
the silence
That reveals your
heart's pain
Of emptiness
Or that great
wrenching-sweet
longing.
That is the time
to try and listen
To what the
Beloved's eyes
most want to say.
-Hafiz

Be Still (surrender)

Be here.
Breathe.
Relax.
Let go.
BEloved.

ponder (go deeper)

Listen to the song, "You Are Loved," sung by Stars Go Dim. You *are* loved. You are glittering in value and worth. Write the words or feelings that pique your attention.

This time to be still is a keenly important one, dear one. Particularly if there is a wound you carry. If so, linger here a bit longer. What are you thinking, feeling, hoping, and longing for? Maybe you don't feel critically wounded, but you are hurt. How do you allow yourself to be human, to feel sad or angry, when you have been injured? Are there ways you pretend or deny that woundedness, feigning that you're good when you're really not? *Be real. Be you.*

Take whatever feels chaotic, painful, or broken in you. Really think about it. Imagine it. What does it look, sound, and feel like? Imagine Spirit, the One, hovering over it like a bird. What happens? Stay here for a moment. Even if nothing happens right now, in your way with your voice, ask for what you really want and need. Ask for an experience of peace and hope to be yours, right here and now. Be expectant. Be watchful. This can be a lifeline. This One is with you, has never left you, loves you with a big love, and can buoy and *enCOURAGE* you throughout each and every season of life.

Are there sacred texts in your life that speak to a promise that gives you hope in the pain? In my spiritual tradition, one of my favorite claims is that God promises to work astonishing good out of unspeakable pain. Even the injustice, the unfair, the abuse, the mistreatment. All of it. Does this give you solace? Is it something for you to walk with, meditate on, and contemplate? Does it give you a flicker of hope?

Engage (commit)

A nudge. Light a candle for a person who is wounded and capturing your heart's attention, whether near or far. *This person may be you.* Allow the flicker of the flame to be an act of prayer or meditation. Imagine the light of this candle warming the wounded one and kindling the flickering flame of hope.

Now, it's your turn. What or who are you beckoned to *commit to, connect with,* or *create*—whether in small or big ways?

Share something from this PoP with someone you trust.

Your Word. Write a word that has captured your attention in this PoP.

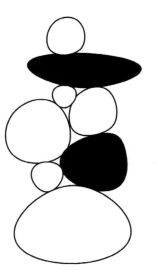

BE BOLD. BE BRAVE. BE YOU.

healing & hurting

Companioning one another
through the small and big hazards that come with life
is one of our great invitations and callings.
We can heal and we can hurt one another
as we go about our day-to-day living.

Our mighty human family can and has perpetuated
grave injustices upon its own members.
And yet, we can be the very hands and feet
that bring healing and hope to one another.

I invite you to simply, yet radically,
reorient your vision and capacity for your part
in the world's great beauty, complexity, and struggles.
In this colossal collective,
you will find the courage and commitment
to excavate and cultivate the gold, the good,
and the glimmering hope
in the midst of the dark.

Choosing

AS YOU BUILD YOUR TRIBE, THIS IS A KEY INVITATION TO BE DISCERNING ABOUT THOSE YOU CHOOSE FOR YOUR INNER CIRCLE OF TRUSTED SOUL FRIENDS.

Do not put on a blindfold and be led on your journey by just anyone.

Any community or tribe is made up of humans, and humans always have flaws and imperfections that can cause injury in either inadvertent or intentional ways. Herein lies a dynamic invitation to live connected and engaged with others in your mighty collective *and* to do so wisely.

You need others
—chosen *careFULLY*—
to walk with you.

Be Still (surrender)

See the feelings, the scars, of the injuries you've received
from others—be they recent or long ago.
See them and let them go.
Close your eyes
and breathe.
Just be.
Open up to whatever you need—
known or unknown.
Breathe it in,
as if you can take in this thing that you most need,
with this breath.
And the next one.
And the next one.

ponder (go deeper)

This song feels like a lullaby to my soul—"Forgiveness," sung by Sandra McCracken. It's
a deeply raw and real song. As you listen to this love song of letting go, sit with the parts
in you that have been wounded by others … or where you've injured yourself. Write about
what comes up, what you desire, and what calls to you.

Ponder and write about an occasion in which you were let down by someone and you
were hurt. What happened? What do you want and need in a trustworthy tribe moving
forward?

Have there been times when humans failed you entirely and the Spirit was present? How did this Presence show up and what was offered? What is it like for you to cultivate this relationship as an essential element of your trusted tribe?

Engage (commit)

A nudge. Write down or imagine the name of a person or an experience that has caused you pain. Play the song, "Forgiveness." Light a candle. Sit with and ask yourself or Spirit if there are any places of burdensome resentment or unforgiveness that confine or shackle you. Ask yourself if it's time to let it go. This is not a *place of should*. But of desire. If you want to, consider doing something as a symbolic act of letting go of this place of burden. Perhaps place the paper with the name on it in a bowl and pour a cup of water over the paper. Imagine that you are washing this pain, this hurt, this person with waters of forgiveness. Write about and watch for any shifts in your energy, in your soul, in your thinking in the days to come. Bask in a moment of infinite tenderness and gentleness towards yourself, wherever you are and whatever you're feeling.

Now, it's your turn. What or who are you beckoned to *commit to, connect with,* or *create*—whether in small or big ways?

Share something from this PoP with someone you trust.

Your Word. Write a word that has captured your attention in this PoP.

BE BOLD. BE BRAVE. BE YOU.

Comparing

THE PRISMATIC BEAUTY OF THIS MIGHTY HUMAN FAMILY IS THAT EACH ONE OF US HAS DISTINCTIVE GIFTS AND INDIVIDUAL WAYS TO OFFER THEM TO THE WORLD.

We cannot wholeheartedly participate in this diverse tribe if we get caught in the hook of comparing our unique strengths and purposes with one another. Some of us are wildly exuberant extroverts, others steadfast introverts.

Some of us may be committed to tend to those closest to us, while others of us feel drawn to support those who live far away. Some of us may have work to do that is visibly significant, while others' work may be quieter in its impact. Our world is full of amazing people doing unbelievably remarkable things that are making a significant difference. We need it all. No one way is better than another.

Comparing sets up all of us for living small, flickering lives. It's an epic and mighty waste of time. We are all in such different places in this journey. Wherever you find yourself, in this moment, right now, I offer a nudge: relax a bit, let go, and pay attention to your own story and your personal longings without determining them better or worse than another's. You may be ready to make small shifts by weaving new ways of feel-good inspired action into your daily life. Or you may have already made, or are about to make, gigantic shifts related to your career, focus, and unstoppable purpose on the planet. Wherever you are is perfect. Choose to live in a way that is unique to you.

Be rooted in the reality that you are deeply valuable
—right here, right now—
as is, not after you do more good
or become more successful.
May crippling comparisons lessen within you,
become quieter, and lose their power.

Wherever you find yourself, in this moment, right now, I offer a nudge: relax a bit, let go, and pay attention to your own story and your personal longings without determining them better or worse than another's.

Live life alone less.
Reach out to your *kula* of soul friends.
Celebrate the glittering gifts
and destinies of those around you.
Do today whatever is yours to do—no more, no less.

You were made for this.

Be Still (surrender)

All is well.
In this place of shhhhh.
You need not do anything.
Allow yourself the gift of *BEing*.
Be silent.
Be quiet.
Rest.
Receive.

ponder (go deeper)

Listen to the song, "Good Life," sung by OneRepublic. As you let go of comparing, this is what is waiting: a *good* life. What images, words, ideas come to you as you hear the words and the rousing music and beat? Write about what you see and hear. Walk a bit, deepening your learnings with each step.

What are the triggers, vulnerabilities, or historical patterns that set you up for comparing yourself with others? Think back to a moment when you were shriveled by a comparison— within yourself or another toward you. Go into detail. How did it feel, what was going on? What could have been different that would have kept you from going down that path of comparisons?

Do you have a pattern of looking at the treasure troves—your perceived "wealth" of oth-ers—in a way that diminishes or makes your own gifts feel worthless, small, or *not* valu-able? If so, write down the statements you use that have historically stopped you from a life of feel-good giving. For example, *I don't have enough. Others have more. If I only had what _____ (name) has, I would be able to do, give, be more.* And now, flip the statements to their reverse. Be a warrior in response to these toxic messages of comparison. Invite the always-present Sacred to fight them for you when you're worn out, to help you understand them in the light of Love.

Engage (commit)

A nudge. Write down a bio, a description of you, in ways that spotlight and describe you as the person you are now—in radiant, *powerFULL*, true ways. Free of comparisons. Free of measuring. Free to *be* and *do* you.

Now, it's your turn. What or who are you beckoned to *commit to*, *connect with*, or *create*—whether in small or big ways?

Share something from this PoP with someone you trust.

Your Word. Write a word that has captured your attention in this PoP.

BE BOLD. BE BRAVE. BE YOU.

Witnessing

IT TAKES COURAGE-LOTS OF IT-TO KEEP IT REAL AND TO ALLOW PEOPLE INTO OUR LESS-THAN-PERFECT MOMENTS.

The imperfections, challenges, and conundrums in EVERYday life offer a plethora of opportunities to learn, to expand, and to deepen our connections with those in our tribe.

It's not always easy. It's often uncomfortable and vulnerable to grow in the company of others. I call this witnessing.

Witnessing is a dynamic commitment to find simple and powerful ways to companion people. This, too, is rooted in the everyday of life. It'll keep you on your toes, with your eyes and heart wide open. Sometimes it means that you champion and celebrate what you see in those around you. At other times, it means you will sit with and say nothing to one who is struggling … just being with another person who is in pain can be a most extraordinary act. They don't need to be alone or hide in a challenging moment. Sometimes it means speaking and calling attention to what a person may not see as a blind spot or a historical pattern that is eclipsing freedom and joy in their life.

There is gold here, in this sweet company.
You will be more free.
Free to be bold. Free to be brave. Free to be you.
And you will usher in the same
freedom, boldness, and bravery
in those around you.

Practicing courage, compassion, and connection in our daily lives is how we cultivate worthiness. The key word is practice. Mary Daly, a theologian, writes, "Courage is like—it's a habitus, a habit, a virtue: You get it by courageous acts. It's like you learn to swim by swimming. You learn courage by couraging."
-Brené Brown, *The Gifts of Imperfection*

Be Still (surrender)

Here we are, again.
At a place of pause.
At a place of being.
No need to do or think about one thing.
Not any to-do's
or need to resolve the past.
Set aside anything other than resting,
being,
breathing, and
opening.
Ahh.

ponder (go deeper)

Listen to the song, "Jump Rope," by Blue October. This life of keeping it real, of boldly being *you*, and of allowing yourself to be witnessed and championed by others is not easy. This song is all about the ups and downs in life, of holding onto hope and trust that you'll find your way. You might want to get up for this song, saunter, or dance a bit. Write what phrases of this song-poem grab you. What parts connect to your life today?

What's coming to mind for you in this chapter? A current or old experience, relationship, dream, or hope? Stay here. Be gentle. Be courageous. Look for what your heart may be longing for or what the Sacred may be trying to heal, reshape, or reframe.

Think back to or imagine a time in which you were hiding, discouraged, or derailed, a time when a tribe member supported you to come on out, in that less-than-perfect moment. Write about your experience. How did they "find" you? How did they encourage you to come out of hiding? What happened as a result of their support?

Engage (commit)

A nudge. Reach out to someone you know in your life who is in hiding, someone who may need you to go and find them, to talk together, hear your perspective and your voice, describing the hope awaiting them. Give them a helping hand to pull them up and walk out of hiding with them.

Now, it's your turn. What or who are you beckoned to *commit to, connect with,* or *create*—whether in small or big ways?

Share something from this PoP with someone you trust.

Your Word. Write a word that has captured your attention in this PoP.

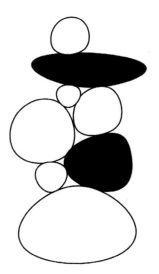

BE BOLD. BE BRAVE. BE YOU.

Lamenting

I THINK ABOUT MY DEAR FRIEND, FATOUMA. FATOUMA'S HEART CRACKED IN TWO WHEN HER SON PASSED AWAY LAST YEAR. HER WAILS OF LAMENT WILL REMAIN IN MY HEART AND EARS FOREVER.

According to her Islamic faith tradition, for forty days of *du'ua*, of prayer and mourning, her tribe of sisters and brothers gathered and encircled her. She did not mourn or pray alone. We lit candles, brought food, prayed, sang, and cried, together.

When it comes to the big stuff, the really hard days, we are not meant to find solutions or care for ourselves alone.

One day, she said to us, "I am a very strong woman, but without you and Allah, peace be upon Him, I wouldn't have made it. There is no doubt in my mind; I wouldn't have made it through this alone. I am African, Muslim, woman, grandma, sister, mother, wife, aunt, friend. Allah, peace be upon Him, gave me everything. He has given me the world as my family. He gave me you."

Her sacred text, the Quran, speaks to this: "And as for the believing men and the believing women, they are guardians of each other; they enjoin good and forbid evil and keep up prayer."

When it comes to the big stuff,
the really hard days,
we are not meant to find solutions
or care for ourselves alone.
The greater the struggle,
the greater the grief,
the more we need each other.
Sometimes, our lives depend on it.

Be Still (surrender)

Sit down.
Lean back, rest your head.
Prop up your feet.
Three breaths,
slow inhales,
deep exhales.
Stay here ... for as long as you can, need, want.

ponder (go deeper)

Listen to the song, "All Through the Night," sung by Sleeping at Last. Write about and explore in your own way what strikes you in this song-poem of being with one another in the midst of the dark nights. If you feel alone in your struggle, consider how this might be a dream or a prayer for support, for companions in the midst of the hard.

Has there been a time when you were the recipient of this tender-loving-care while in the depths of despair? Was it easy or difficult to accept? Think on or write about the details—the feelings, the place, the response in you to it all.

Has there been a time of great sorrow in your life when you felt alone? Perhaps you didn't feel comfortable reaching out to others for the support you needed. What made it difficult for you to ask for support? If that time is now, sit with this nudge: Is there one person you can call, text, or email today? Right here, is there one person with whom you can share your raw and real story?

Engage (commit)

A nudge. Set a date to gather some folks to explore and dream together how you might extend some care to someone or a community in need of support.

Now, it's your turn. What or who are you beckoned to *commit to, connect with,* or *create*—whether in small or big ways?

Share something from this PoP with someone you trust.

Your Word. Write a word that has captured your attention in this PoP.

BE BOLD. BE BRAVE. BE YOU.

look for & find

To those who feel vulnerable, invisible, lost, silenced,
hungry, hopeless, or hurting—
we hear and see you.

We are coming and are gathering many more,
each claiming and using
our unique purpose on the planet
to be with you, to enCOURAGE,
listen to, collaborate,
and learn from you.

We pledge to do whatever we can.
We do not have the answers,
but we are committed to a life with you
in which we cultivate hope and a future.
You are not alone.
You are not invisible.
Crying may remain for a night, but joy is coming.

YOU DO NOT NEED TO DIG DEEP TO FIND PAIN IN OUR WORLD.

Most likely, steady streams of ticker tape lines scroll across the bottom of your TV screen and your cell phone chimes with news updates of the horrifying and the unimaginable.

What to do? You know that these challenges are mighty, and you may feel at a loss for what you can possibly do to make a difference.

You may be nudged to move toward what beckons—and maybe what breaks—your heart. This takes courage. You've got this, because you guessed it—you're not alone.

In the stories to come, witness the courage and commitment of those who chose to wade into the deep of the pain in our world. Despite the crush and the deep pain, the arc of each of these stories is aglow with inspiration, hope, and great big love.

May you find a bit more of what matters to you in the stories that follow.

Called to Craters

IT WAS 1992, DURING THE SIEGE OF SARAJEVO. IN NEARLY FOUR YEARS, TEN THOUSAND PEOPLE WERE KILLED IN THE CITY OF SARAJEVO, THE CAPITAL OF BOSNIA AND HERZEGOVINA.

One day, in the midst of the conflict, cellist Vedran Smailović received word that twenty-two fellow citizens had been bombed. They died waiting in line for bread.

Tragic. Terrifying. Unjust. Unfair.

It would be understandable if he went home and stayed there, behind locked doors, as long as he could. The world outside was on fire, terror-stricken, and there was little hope in sight. But that is not what he did. No, Vedran did something extraordinary that is still being talked about today, more than two decades later. He went home, packed up his cello, and stepped out his door. He was on a mission. With cello in hand, he walked to where the bomb had fallen, planted himself in the crater left by the bomb in the midst of the rubble, and began to play. He called this act a *protest in the darkness*, and he returned daily, for twenty-two days, in memoriam of each person who had died.

The cello was a simple, *EVERYday*, ordinary object for Vedran. In the face of unimaginable and continuous death and destruction, he picked up his tool, gave what he could, and tended to what was right in front of him.

You also have a one-of-a-kind gift and purpose. You might even think of it as a unique song you sing or a tool you wield as you move through your days. Whatever it might be, you have something that will bring beauty, companionship, or meaning into the bomb craters and war zones of the lives of those around you.

Do you know what your "cello tool" is or can you hear your unique song yet? Have you not sung a word or a note yet, or have you been chanting it your whole life, quietly or at the top of your lungs? Listen for the melody.

Pause. Listen. Wait. Look. Pay attention. The melody will come.

May the notes you play and sing
awaken and light you up,
enCOURAGE others, and
energize you with pulsing purpose
today and each and every day to come.

Play your song. Sing it.
Experience the notes, lilting and deep,

> In the face of unimaginable and continuous death and destruction, he picked up his tool, gave what he could, and tended to what was right in front of him.

loud and soft.
There is none like it on earth.
Never has been and never will be.
Do not compare it with another.
Do not hide it or try to whisper it.
Allow your notes to join the chorus.

You will bring
beauty, light, love, and hope
to the craters.

Be Still (surrender)

Bask in the sound of silence.
This soul-nourishing quiet time.
It is for you, only and deeply for you.
Relax. Soften. Let go.
Be, just be.

ponder (go deeper)

Listen to the song, "Why It Matters," sung by the amazing Sara Groves. This song was inspired by the story of Vedran Smailović, often called "The Cellist of Sarajevo." In this song, Sara sings about the places of chaos, confusion, and brokenness—which are plentiful in our world—*and* why beauty matters so very much in those very places. As you hear the song, pay attention to a word or phrase that captures your attention. What is the connection to your life? How does it inspire, encourage, or nudge you today?

What bomb craters are capturing your attention right now? Who inspires you, who are the people you see who are doing work in the bomb craters, protesting darkness, and bringing beauty to places of destruction in your community or world? What do you love about what they do, how they do it, where they are working? (Be on the lookout for times when this shifts from igniting inspiration to crippling comparison.)

Do you hear or dream of a new song with new melodies? Do you see ways it can speak to, be present to, and wade into the deep where people are in pain? How might you explore ways to harmonize and collaborate with others? Take a moment to imagine a chorus, your song joining with others. How does that feel? What is the sound of the harmonies? What notes are needed in your life to make this singing more full and complete?

Engage (commit)

A nudge. Reach out to a stranger or friend today who inspires you in the ways they work in the hard places of the world, bringing beauty to bomb craters.

Now, it's your turn. What or who are you beckoned to *commit to, connect with,* or *create*—whether in small or big ways?

Share something from this PoP with someone you trust.

Your Word. Write a word that has captured your attention in this PoP.

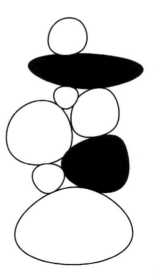

BE BOLD. BE BRAVE. BE YOU.

purpose in pain

CLUES TO YOUR PURPOSE ON THE PLANET MAY BE SITTING RIGHT NEXT TO YOUR PAIN.

Christina Noble's life depicts just that. Breathtaking in resilience, her life of *comPASSIONate* commitment has made life better for nearly a million children far away from the country of her birth.

Her life hasn't been easy. No, far from it. Before her story today of extraordinary impact, she navigated many years of excessive struggle. It was brutal and her heart was broken. More than once.

Born in Ireland in 1944, her mother died when she was ten, her father was held in the grip of alcoholism, and the family descended deeply into poverty. Christina and her siblings picked through garbage dumps for their food. As is too often the case in the world, violence shadowed her vulnerability, and she was raped as a teenager. Once married, her husband physically and emotionally abused her.

Gut-wrenching. Unfair. Unjust.

Though it seemed this was her devastating lot in life and there was nothing she could do to change it, mercifully, this was not the end of her story. She tenaciously persevered, step by challenging step.

As a teenager, in the midst of days of tremendous trials, she had a dream one night of a distant land, Vietnam. She knew next to nothing about the country. So, although curious about its message, Christina tucked this dream into her heart, not to be explored again for many years.

Twenty years later, she bought a one-way plane ticket to Vietnam, fueled by a hunch and a hope that embedded in that teenage dream was a clue to her destiny. The very day she landed, her heart was immediately captured by the children on the street.

> Her dreams, destiny, and joy were nestled right alongside her personal pain and struggle. (So are yours.)

Her birth country of Ireland and Vietnam were far away from each other, with very different cultures. But she quickly discovered that the vulnerable poor children in both places were not so dissimilar. Remembering her own impoverished childhood, she understood their hunger as she saw them picking through garbage and knew their susceptibility to those who could exploit their vulnerability as they wandered the streets.

A fire was lit in Christina that has fueled a movement of jaw-dropping support of nearly one million vulnerable children. The Christina Noble Children's Foundation (cncf. org) provides access to education, healthcare, safe living environments, and a future illuminated by hope. Her work has expanded beyond Vietnam and today includes Mongolia.

To be sure, looking at Christina's story from a big picture vantage point, it appears epic in its impact and scope. Yet, the grand story began with small and simple steps. Despite great personal struggles, she kept walking. She didn't run away from her heartache. She dared to remember and trust that the dream she'd had as a teenager held a clue for her destiny. She waded into the deep to get close to the street children of Vietnam. And there, right there, she found the joy of a life of oceanic purpose and love.

Her dreams, destiny, and joy
were
nestled
right
alongside
her personal pain and struggle.
(So are yours.)

Be Still (surrender)

Peace. Peace.
Inhale peace, quiet, rest.
Exhale all that burdens and encumbers.
Smile gently and softly.
Your only thing to do here
is be.
Be.

ponder (go deeper)

Listen to (and watch the video, if you can) "Wavin' Flag – Celebration Mix," sung by K'NAAN. His poetry-song has this thread of growing older, getting stronger, fighting for freedom. Does this song have any treasures for you today?

This is an epic story. I'm curious, my friend, what strikes you, what calls to you? Did any part of Christina's story give you goose-bumps or bring tears to your eyes, connect with your own story?

Our great joy, destiny, and dream often sit right next to our greatest fear, our deepest sorrow. Are there connections you can make between injustices and hurt in your life and a passion to serve and work with people who have experienced something similar? Dig a bit deeper by writing or exploring it in your own way.

Engage (commit)

A nudge. Take one step towards a current or old dream. This dream may be one you had, literally while you were asleep, or be one that has been in you for a long time. Trust that it may provide some clues to your destiny, your purpose on the planet. Do one thing today to cultivate a connection to this dream. Do one thing to add fuel to the flame of your story. *Bonus nudge:* Watch the movie, *Noble*, about Christina's life. Pay attention to what captures your attention.

Now, it's your turn. What or who are you beckoned to *commit to, connect with,* or *create*—whether in small or big ways?

Share something from this PoP with someone you trust.

Your Word. Write a word that has captured your attention in this PoP.

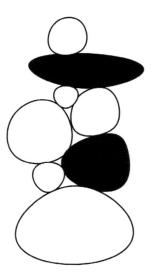

BE BOLD. BE BRAVE. BE YOU.

New Stories

WHEN YOU OFFER YOUR GIFTS-YOURSELF-TO THE WORLD, BREATHTAKING AND ASTONISHING THINGS HAPPEN.

The extraordinary powers of restoration and transformation out of seemingly dead-end stories often emerge as we become kindling companions and fuel for one another on the road. This is one of the most essential parts of life's adventure.

That's exactly what happened when an unlikely collaboration was forged between a tribe of surfers and veterans. *Resurface* is a remarkable film that tells the story of their inspiring partnership in response to a very real and serious need (resurfacethemovie.com).

The film states that in the U.S., twenty-two veterans kill themselves every twenty-four hours (and those are *only* the reported ones). In *Resurface,* the veterans speak of gut-wrenching struggles, of bodies being damaged by bombs and shrapnel, of spirits being crushed, and of tremendous guilt, pain, and hopelessness, without dreams for the future. In this film, we see how a community of surfers *waded into the deep* of this pain and committed to companion these men and women. In and out of the ocean, with Operation Surf, we see the lives of veterans ignited and renewed. The film portrays how the waves and this community collective have begun to wash away despondency and isolation. Seeds have been planted for a renewed vision for a *good life*.

We witness stories of surfers and veterans finding purpose and buoyant new stories, together. In the surfing and service. In the giving and receiving. In the purpose and pain. Do you see it, hear it, feel it? These individuals offered what they had, from where they were, in the ways they could. This way of life is one of pulsing purpose and plentiful new beginnings.

It's not only these brave veterans who need this restoring reset, though. There are times, seasons, and days when each one of us needs a new story, with changed habits, memories, and patterns of thought and action. Be courageously honest about where you are and what pain exists in your life. It has the potential to illuminate your next steps and leaps. Bit by bit, your gaze and your path will become clearer, sharper, and more powerful than ever.

Out of heartbreak,
your roots will grow,
strengthened by love,
to cultivate green, growing things,
healing in you … and in others.

Out of heartbreak,
your roots will grow,
strengthened by love,
to cultivate green, growing things,
healing in you …
and in others.

Be Still (surrender)

Breathe in as deeply as you can.
Again.
Puff out your chest.

Exhale till every drop of air is gone.
Draw your chin softly toward your heart.
Soften your jaw, your brow.
Bask.
Rest.
Be.

ponder (go deeper)

Listen to (and watch the video, if you can) "Stand By Me," sung by Playing for Change. This is an anthem of togetherness in the midst of the pain, the dark, the fear. *Ponder* and write about the ahas that come your way.

Are you in a season when you need to be supported by a few folks around you? Are you intrigued or do you long to describe yourself with a new story? In what parts of yourself or your life is this desire for a new story beckoning? Close your eyes for a moment and imagine your life in this new-story-place. What does it look like? What do you look like? Who is with you? Write it. Draw it.

Are you filled up enough and nudged to give a bit or a bunch to those around you from a place of plenty? Is there someone in your life who seems to be stuck in a sad, painful, or old story? Might you wade into the deep with them, cultivating purpose and buoyant new stories, together?

Do you have a physical activity that brings peace, hope, and healing as you do it? Surfing works some mighty magic for many of the veterans in Operation Surf. What might you begin to do or commit to do more regularly in your life?

If you don't yet have something that fosters such feelings within you, spend some time sitting with the idea and see what you hear that might surprise and delight you. Talk, brainstorm, dream with a trusted person or the Sacred.

Engage (commit)

A nudge. As if on a treasure hunt, connect one dot in your life between what you love or an area of expertise you have and a need in the world. Send one email, make one phone call, do one thing that will fuel this curiosity. Consider and be inspired by the dots connected in the above collaboration between surfers and veterans.

Now, it's your turn. What or who are you beckoned to *commit to, connect with,* or *create*—whether in small or big ways?

Share something from this PoP with someone you trust.

Your Word. Write a word that has captured your attention in this PoP.

BE BOLD. BE BRAVE. BE YOU.

Dignity from Dust

SHE IS HANDED A BLACK ROUND THING. HER HEART IS BEATING FAST BECAUSE SHE KNOWS WHAT THIS IS. A BOMB. HER NAME IS HANNAH.

She is eight years old, and she has no choice but to carry it. The year is 2003, and the Maoist rebels have been hiding out in her village in Nepal.

It's the ideal location, as not many care about her people, called the *Badi* (pronounced "body"). They have been legally categorized, since 1854, as *Pani Na Chalne* ("Impure and Untouchable") in Nepal's legal code. They are a despised people—the lowest ranked untouchable caste in western Nepal, called by many the "untouchables among the untouchables" and the "dust of Nepal." The Maoists figure they are safely invisible living among these *untouchables*, this *dust*.

"Careful," he tells her. "One wrong move and you'll blow up. You'll be dead."

Hannah knows this story well. She has been told what to do her whole life. As have her sisters, mother, and grandmothers. They are Badi women. They know what they cannot do: walk, eat, or drink with people of higher cultural standing and caste. No one wants to be near them, to touch them, to walk on the same village path as them … until it comes to sex. When sex is desired, these *untouchable* Badi women become very *touchable*.

It hasn't always been such a struggle. The Badi haven't always been disdained and sexually objectified. Her people were esteemed artists in the courts of the kings of Nepal. Hannah's mother danced for the king. Their very name, *Badi*, means "musical people." But, over time, this gift was slowly perverted; so much so that Badi women have become lucrative objects sought after for sex trafficking and are taken to brothels throughout Asia, where they live enslaved for many years. Most are never permitted to leave. Some girls are kept in their villages in Nepal, where men crawl through their windows, asserting their right to have sex with them. "No" has not been a permissible

> Hope is being able to see that there is light despite all of the darkness.
> -Desmond Tutu

answer. Submission to the power of men and of others in higher castes has been the only way for women in this people group. That is, until recently.

The same girl who trudged through the jungle, with hands trembling as the bomb lay nestled in her fingers, living each day perpetually at risk of being sexually exploited, is leading a movement of her own people that is changing the future of many. Hannah now travels the globe, speaking about her life and opening people's hearts to the realities of injustice in the world. She invites listeners to wake up and join the fight for freedom for all.

Because of Hannah and her community's collective vision and activism, a growing number of Badi women are being rescued from brothels, and many others have been spared from the horrors of sex trafficking for the first time in generations. Many Badi girls and boys are going to school, takings steps and leaps towards futures full-to-the-brim with purpose and possibility. They have more freedoms than ever before and are rising from the ashes. A new story is being kindled, and the glow of hope is brighter than ever.

Hannah is a leader, a COURAGEous warrior of love.
She inspires and awakens.
She has ignited not only the women of Nepal,
but countless others
with her passion to set the world ablaze with hope.

Today, Hannah is free,
dancing her way through life,
whirling around the world,
sharing stories and inviting us to join her as sisters and brothers,
to flood the dark places in the world with light, together.

The same girl who trudged through the jungle, with hands trembling as the bomb lay nestled in her fingers, living each day perpetually at risk of being sexually exploited, is leading a movement of her own people that is changing the future of many.

Be Still (surrender)

Yes, pause here.
Especially pause here,
in these moments following a story with elements
of great pain and injustice.
There is hope.
And, here, there is peace.
There is a chance to be free of any burden to carry,
to worry,
to do anything other than be.
Be, breathe.
Exhale, let go.

ponder (go deeper)

Listen to "Beautiful Things," sung by Gungor. It is bursting with hope, images of growing things out of dust, and life out of ashes. Ponder and write about what moves and captivates you in this soul-rich song.

Where do you feel powerless, voiceless, impoverished … low in hope? Do you find any part of your story here? Was there a time when you felt voiceless, less-than-free, or struggling to survive? Write about this experience in the past or present.

What do you know about human trafficking? How do these epic injustices feel to you? If it has terrified you, how might it feel different to connect to Hannah's story, which is so full of hope and healing, rather than the "cause" of human trafficking? Consider how other global "issues" might shift their magnitude by connecting with individual stories and storytellers. Are there big struggles that matter greatly to you that you can chunk down into smaller bites like this, such that you have a way to think about, maybe even participate in, anew?

Engage (commit)

A nudge. Light a candle as an act of kindling the light in the places of darkness in the world. Meditate, send some juju, or pray about the abhorrent global reality of human trafficking … or another challenge in the world that captures your attention. Envision some rays of love and hope penetrating the darkness, bringing freedom and justice, and raising up people to join the fight. (Maybe *you* will be one of those raised up to fight…)

Now, it's your turn. What or who are you beckoned to *commit to*, *connect with*, or *create*—whether in small or big ways?

Share something from this PoP with someone you trust.

Your Word. Write a word that has captured your attention in this PoP.

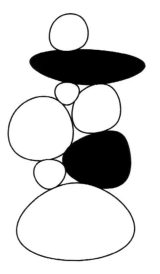

BE BOLD. BE BRAVE. BE YOU.

Hope's Glow

HOPE IS *NEEDED* AND IT IS *FLOURISHING* AROUND THE WORLD, IN NEIGHBORHOODS, VILLAGES, REFUGEE CAMPS, AND WAR ZONES.

For me, at the peak of my eating disorder and during other everyday human struggles, hope was there. I was never alone.

Even when I couldn't see hope or my companions clearly through my squinting, tired eyes, it flickered. Even when I couldn't hear, feel, or sense much of anything good, hope was alive. At those times, the world—and my life—seemed so very, very dark. But even in the midst of those dim days, there was a spark that never went out, a nudge not to give up that was lodged in my heart. Hope was glowing beyond what I could see. It sat right next to, within, and around the struggle and pain.

Do you feel it, do you see it too? Are addiction, brokenness, and pain present in your own life and in the lives of those you love? Do you feel bits or a bunch of shame, fear, sorrow, and darkness within and around you? Does the unimaginable injustice in the world seem greater than the hope? Does it seem that nightmares are stronger than dreams?

Within the struggle, the pain, the broken—even before you see or feel it—hope is present. Take heart and know the struggle will not last forever. Sometimes hope is particularly hard to see, but it is there. The fear, darkness, and struggles that are in the world or within you may be massive, but they are trumped by love and light and hope—always.

Let's together commit
not to give up or label any place or person as hopeless,
to bring hope's rays to bear in places that many would say are beyond its reach,
to look for, find, and kindle hope's glow, even when it is just a tiny flicker.

> The fear, darkness, and struggles that are in the world or within you may be massive, but they are trumped by love and light and hope—always.

The darker the places and the greater the heartbreak,
the more we need hope and each other.
There are endless flickers of hope,
no matter how dark the day,
for you and for our entire common human family.

Be Still (surrender)

In the pain, pause.
In the heartbreak, pause.
Whether you feel a flicker of hope or feel nothin', pause.
Breathe deep, full, big breaths.
Breathing in hope.
Breathing in love. Breathing in peace.
Stay here for a few more minutes.

ponder (go deeper)

Listen to "Glory," sung by John Legend and Common. This is a song of freedom, of dignity, of fighting for justice with others … a movement of many. Listen for the themes of everyday people doing their part.

Where are the flickers of hope in the world and in your own heart? How might you stoke the fire of hope, of beauty, even in the hard—even in the pain—in your life challenges or challenges in the world that you are aware of?

Take whatever feels hopeless in or around you. Really think about it. Imagine it. What does it look, sound, feel like? Imagine a glow of some goodness entering into the hopelessness … a light, a seed planted and growing, a song of beauty, a shout of truth, a small act with great love. Invite Spirit to be there and to plant in you a seed of hope today. In your way with your voice, write about and ask for a glimpse or a sense of hope's glow. Even if you feel nothing exceptional right now, be expectant. Be watchful.

Engage (commit)

A nudge. Reach out to one person today who needs a bit of hope's glow. A stranger or a friend. Someone near or far.

Now, it's your turn. What or who are you beckoned to *commit to, connect with,* or *create*—whether in small or big ways?

Share something from this PoP with someone you trust.

Your Word. Write a word that has captured your attention in this PoP.

BE BOLD. BE BRAVE. BE YOU.

3

[sparking]

glimmering. inspiring. activating or
inciting. setting off a sudden force.

It's time to explore and discover
a more sparking and sparkling way of living.

This is the living ablaze way.
It is fierce and whole,
fueled more than ever by your purpose on the planet,
kindled by connections with those
in your mighty human family near and far.
Step, leap, and dance your way
into new ways to offer your gifts to the world.

Get ready to see the stunning ways you and your tribe
will, together, make a mighty difference.
PowerFULLY together.

one-of-a-kind

You are here with a destiny that is
one-of-a-kind in nature.
There's no one like you—never has been,
never will be.
This is your *superPOWER*.
Open up to the truth, claim it, share it.

Until you express your one-of-a-kind destiny
in thought, word, and deed,
the world will not see or benefit
from its stunning gift.

When you do, you will be living
—really living—
in that edge-of-your-seat sort of a way.

Waiting for you

LIVING A LIT UP, SPARKING LIFE, NEED NOT BE DEPENDENT ON KNOWING AND SEEING CLEARLY THE PATH FORWARD.

It does not require you to wholly understand your gifts, your destiny, or your why. It is not dependent upon a sense of potent proficiency. Perhaps this is the most *needed nudge* thus far.

A deeply natural and exceedingly common human tendency is to believe that living with good juju and feelings like joy, peace, and confidence requires lots of other accomplishments first. But it's not true. This way of life is not *out there* in the future or dependent on you doing anything first. A full-to-the brim experience of a daily life *sparking* with feel-good meaning and purpose can be yours here and can be part of your daily life now, in the midst of the not-yet-known, the not-yet-understood, and the not-yet-proficient. You can walk through life, your head held high with confidence, even amidst these not-yet bits.

This is good news. Your value, your worth, and your purpose are planted in you. They reside in you. They are yours. Right here and right now.

If you don't know your exact next steps, your whys, your hows, or your whats, not to worry. They're coming. When you see your next step, take it.

My friend, keep walking. Don't give up. Don't lose heart. Don't quit.

Keep cultivating places where you can be yourself,
claim your unique passions and purpose,
find ways to collaborate with others,
and boldly build these rhythms of PoPs into your day-to-day life,
taking time to fuel yourself from deep within.

This way of life will become as effortless as the thrumming of your heart.

> This is good news. Your value, your worth, and your purpose are planted in you. They reside in you. They are yours. Right here and right now.

Be Still (surrender)

Buzzzzz.
Our brains often zing at lightning speed.
Our bodies can endeavor to keep up with
the endless lists, needs, and opportunities.

But here, invite the buzzing,
the zinging,
to stop.

Here, there is peace,
there is rest.
Just breathe and be.

ponder (go deeper)

Listen to (and watch the video, if you can) "Hey, Hey, Hey," sung by Michael Franti and Spearhead. This song is for you. It's a big and powerful song, poetically proclaiming that you are here with one life, that nothing is impossible. Write about what captures your attention in the lyrics, in the music, in the invitation to not let your life's moments slip away.

What are some things, people, or places you love—hobbies, places you've visited in the past, people you've met, or things you dream of doing in the future? Go for a walk and speak into a voice memo in your phone or write about it, with as much detail as you can muster. Pay attention to how you feel, where your thoughts go, and amble on this path for a bit. Stoke the fire of your heart's desire—there is a treasure here.

Imagine for a bit: What is the difference you dream of making? If all of the money, time, and talent in the world were yours to make this thing happen, what does it look like? What are you doing? With whom are you working and whom are you serving? Where do you live?

How are you feeling about your *kula* of soul friends? Do you have a place or two where you can be yourself? Where are those places? And with whom? Do you need more spaces like this, where you can keep it wholly real and be you?

Read the free verse that set up this PoP, as modified below, a few times. Play with the tempo and the volume. Whisper it. Then get loud, really loud. After you do, write or go for a walk, pondering the words that most speak to you.

I commit to keep walking.
I'm not giving up. I'm not losing heart. I'm not quitting.

I am cultivating places where I can be myself,
claiming my unique passions and purpose,
finding ways to collaborate with others,
and boldly building these rhythms of PoPs into my day-to-day life,
taking time to fuel myself from deep within.

This way of life is becoming as effortless
as the thrumming of my heart.

Engage (commit)

A nudge. What are a few of your greatest passions … and what are a few places of challenge or brokenness in the world that most capture your attention? Are there two dots that you might connect? Go on a treasure hunt online or in conversations with your friends who are good at brainstorming. Do one thing to expand this connection a bit. Let go of needing to see exactly how it will all work. Just explore a bit and see what happens.

Now, it's your turn. What or who are you beckoned to *commit to, connect with,* or *create*—whether in small or big ways?

Share something from this PoP with someone you trust.

Your Word. Write a word that has captured your attention in this PoP.

BE BOLD. BE BRAVE. BE YOU.

Treasure Hunt

TREES WHISPER. A BREEZE BLOWS. I AM SIX YEARS OLD. MY AUNT DEBY AND I ARE HAVING AN OUTDOOR TEA PARTY.

We wear floppy hats, sip tea, and imagine we are in England, at the palace with the queen. Her pretend British accent lilts and tickles my ears. It is the first memory I have of an accent, and right then and there, I am captivated.

As I grew, so did my curiosity and passion to surround myself with people from all around the world. I posted *National Geographic* pictures and world maps on my walls in my childhood bedroom. They hung from my ceiling and covered my door. These images were of distant lands and communities—of food, homes, and villages I'd not yet seen. I would go to sleep and wake up thinking about these people and places. Even then—in my early days of life—I dreamt that I would see, visit, eat with, and get to know these strangers in distant lands.

Years later, as a teenager, I was offered the extraordinary opportunity to go to India. I basked in the sounds of new languages and blaring horns I heard as I got off the plane in Calcutta, the wave of hot air that hit my skin as I exited the airport, the sensation of wearing saris, the mode of traveling around the city in rickshaws, the smells of aromatic spices coming from the street food vendors at every corner, and the *deLIGHT* to my senses of steaming, sweet, spicy, and milky chai.

From the very start, I felt at home. Back then, it was a bit of a mystery. I found myself thinking, *How can it be, that a place so unfamiliar, so different, feels like home?* But, now, I know why. I understand. This bewildering familiarity and joy were clues pointing to my purpose.

I see how that passion was being sparked and stoked years earlier, in my first memory of an accent with Aunt Deby … as I ripped out magazine pages and wallpapered my room with people and life from all over the world … when I got on a plane bound for India as a teenager. Such simple, *EVERYday*, and important clues for the treasure hunt of my life.

Step by step,
year by year,
the sparks would be set more ablaze,
the distance would lessen,
and these faraway people and I
would connect
and
claim
one
another
as
family.

This bewildering familiarity and joy were clues pointing to my purpose.

Be Still (surrender)

The world is big.
The needs are great.
The treasure hunt is riveting.
But, here and now,
let it all go.
If a burden or worry comes to mind,
imagine exhaling it out.
Just for now.
One by one, exhale each and every thing that comes to mind.
Cultivate silence.
Quiet.
Stillness.
Be.

ponder (go deeper)

Listen to "Amazing Grace," with Ladysmith Black Mambazo and Paul Simon. Let the beauty of these voices wash over you. *Ahh.* What bubbles up in you as you listen to this song?

My friend, what have you loved for a long time? What beckoned your attention as a kid that might be part of the treasure hunt of your life as you know it now … a piece of what has always been a part of you? Imagine. Go back. What did you love to play, what did you love to do, what images, movies, and books captured your imagination? Be curious about those early years and explore what comes up.

Even here, as we're picking up the tempo, remember to go in a soulful, discerning, *bistari* way. The timing always ends up working out just right. Be fueled to move toward and accomplish mighty things, at a time that is just right for you. *Ponder* and write about what it's like to be in this place of exploring and investigation without forcing, pushing, or stressing. How is this tempo different from past ways of being and doing that you've experienced?

Engage (commit)

A nudge. Research a bit today and put in your calendar a time to go to a lecture, watch a movie, listen to a podcast, or start reading a book that will stoke the fire that is sparking in you. Have fun, explore, and go for it!

Now, it's your turn. What or who are you beckoned to *commit to*, *connect with*, or *create*—whether in small or big ways?

Share something from this PoP with someone you trust.

Your Word. Write a word that has captured your attention in this PoP.

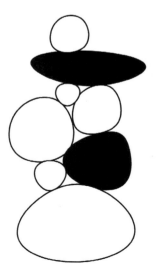

BE BOLD. BE BRAVE. BE YOU.

What's in a Name?

SOMETIMES YOU CAN LOOK TO WHAT HAS BEEN GIVEN TO YOU, WHAT YOU DIDN'T CHOOSE, AND FIND HINTS THAT WILL INFORM AND EXPRESS WHO YOU ARE, MAYBE EVEN UNCOVERING A BIT MORE OF WHAT MATTERS TO YOU.

My name is one of those things. Although I didn't choose it, much of what I love and clues to my destiny are portrayed in mine: Sarah Jane Davison-Tracy[-Badi]. Each word offers a glimpse of my heartbeat and connections that pulse with purpose.

Sarah means "princess of God." My identity has been rooted and grown in the presence of this One who is closer to me than my breath and who guides me each step of the way. My godmother, *Jane*, taught me about the ways in which storytelling is a crucial part of community life, as it is here that we have the opportunity to remind each other of the good and the true, both now and in years past.

Davison is my husband's family name. In our days of engagement, as Brandon and I envisioned and made plans for our life *together*, even then, I knew that words—our names—mattered. Brandon and I both changed our last names, as a reminder that *together* we were different. My maiden name, *Tracy,* is a good ol' Irish name. It speaks to my early roots of tribe. My parents were my first elders, and they are so very wise, and my two remarkable sisters gave me my first taste of the joy that soul sisters bring.

In essence—albeit not legally—my final last name is *Badi.* This name has its roots in a memorable walk on a dusty, breezy, 110-degree blazing hot day in Nepal. My sister Hannah thanked me for coming to her village, for listening, for walking, for spending time with her neighbors and her family—with those she loves. She then gave me my newest last name. "Sarah *didi* (which means "sister" in Nepali)," she said, "You are now one of us. You are a Badi. Your name is now Sarah Badi."

We can do this, as a tribe and family. We can grow one another: new names, identities, and stories beckon.

Just like that, I grew.
Hannah expanded my name—expanded me—that day.

We can do this, as a tribe and family.
We can grow one another:
new names,
identities,
and stories beckon.

Be Still (surrender)

Yes, new things await.
New things are here.
But, for now, let them go.
For now, be still.
Stay here,
for as many moments as you can spare.

ponder (go deeper)

Listen to "Love Rescue Me," sung by U2. Also, find and listen to the fantastic version by the Omagh Community Youth Choir. This song speaks about being without a name, of shame, and conquering the past. It invokes new beginnings. *Ponder* and write about the words and rhythms meant for you.

What hints can you gather from the places you came from, from the people you have lived with—those who have loved you or those who have caused you pain? What clues can you glean from your name that speak to your purpose? What hints does your name give you as to what matters to you? Write a bit about how your name expresses who you are.

Are there names you call yourself or ways your identity is smaller, more limiting, not quite suiting who you know yourself to be? In my spiritual tradition, there are many stories in which God gives a new name to one who is in need of an identity change. If this draws you in, spend some time in dialogue with the Sacred, walking, writing, or listening for a divinely-inspired name change.

Engage (commit)

A nudge. Have a conversation with someone you trust today, someone who has known you for a long time, and ask them to share their insights about what they see as intrinsic aspects of you. Write down and ponder a bit what they share. What excites you? What intrigues you?

Now, it's your turn. What or who are you beckoned to *commit to*, *connect with*, or *create*—whether in small or big ways?

Share something from this PoP with someone you trust.

Your Word. Write a word that has captured your attention in this PoP.

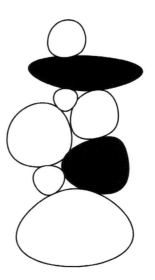

BE BOLD. BE BRAVE. BE YOU.

gathering momentum

Your heart, right now, is beating.
— thrum, thrum, thrum —
It just happens,
effortlessly.
It is — you are — pulsing with life.

My heart quickens now.
— thrum, thrum —
imagining you at this point in your jOURney,
connecting more wholly
with your mighty human family.

Some are near, others far.
Some speak your tongue,
others speak different languages.
In the midst of all that is distinctively different,
we are inextricably interconnected.
— thrum, thrum —

Riding the Wave

I ACCIDENTALLY FELL IN LOVE WITH SURFING A FEW YEARS AGO WHEN I STUMBLED ON A LITTLE-KNOWN AND AMAZING SURF BREAK WHILE ON A RETREAT. IT REMAINS ONE OF THE HAPPIEST ACCIDENTS OF MY LIFE.

Over and over, I have received numerous nuggets of insight from surf instructors. What they have shared with me has profoundly impacted and informed my life ... on and off my board.

In Costa Rica, my buddy Helberth has been surfing since he learned to walk. I love this *hermano* (Spanish for "brother"). He offers simple—and *not* easy—insights in between surf sets. His wise words would often send me scrambling to write them down in my journal at the end of our *sesh*, before I forgot them.

I remember one morning when Helberth suggested I try something new. "*Sarita* (Spanish for "Princess"), why don't you try to switch up your stance on the board?" Moving between your right and left foot as the source of powerful leading on the surfboard is called *switchfoot*. I've since learned that all kinds of fantastic things—versatility, balance, and flexibility—come with practicing switchfoot on a board. But the first few times I tried it, I experienced none of those things. I was sloppy and terribly awkward. It seemed virtually impossible. I'm still not able to switchfoot with finesse and grace.

There are times when I play with the idea of *switchfooting* in my day-to-day life and challenge myself to shift from what's comfortable, what's easier, and *how I've always done it,* to something new. For many years, my source of *powerful leading* was in *doing*. Doing was my primary *stance* as I surfed through life.

If I neglect regular rhythms of PoPs, I get overly rigid in this doing. I find myself on a frenetic hamster wheel. I stay up too late at night and get up too early in the morning. There is little rest and few moments of pause. My brow becomes furrowed, my gut gets

> There are times when I play with the idea of *switchfooting* in my day-to-day life and challenge myself to shift from what's comfortable, what's easier, and how I've always done it, to something new.

tight, and my movements become too rapid. I overschedule myself and leave little-to-no margin to *be*. Here, the messages to *try harder* and *not enough* prevail.

When I don't switchfoot out of this stance, I wipe out. Hard. It's only a matter of time. Game-changing nuggets of wisdom are always found within my PoPs and from my *kula*. Each and every time I reach out to my tribe after a wipeout, they pick me up and cheer for me to keep on going … even when I feel I've got nothin'—or worse, that I *am* nothin'. I find that my need to strive diminishes. I often hear a whisper of next steps, and the flames of hope spark. I'm fueled more by love and less by fear. With more love, the *DOing* is different. *Life is good* in this place.

Yes, this switchfooting is powerful stuff, a force for feel-good change. So, my friend, if you are inclined to overdo, if you find yourself pressed, often running late or up too late, try this switchfoot and be still a bit more. Watch for patterns in your thoughts and actions that tell you the more you do, the more valuable you are. This is one of the biggest and most destructive messages in our human experience. *Switchfoot* it and be free of that burdensome belief.

You have great worth,
you are valuable,
you are loved
because of who you are,
not because of what you do.

Bask in it and believe it.

Be Still (surrender)

There is no need to switchfoot right now.
No need to change anything up.
No need to do anything.
Here, you need only be.
Here, you are loved.
Here, you have great value.
Here, you belong.
Let go.
Breathe.
Be.

ponder (go deeper)

Listen to the song, "Home," sung by Phillip Phillips. My friend, be at home here, rest, fuel up. Don't fear the unknown, the feelings of overwhelm, the messiness of life. *Ponder*, write, and perhaps go for a walk and consider what comes to you here, in the reality of your life today.

What would feel good to *switchfoot* a bit or a lot in your life—old patterns of self-talk, of how you relate to others, of how you start and end your days, of how you engage with the Sacred, or something else entirely? Write about what comes to you. Imagine moving through life in this new way, changing up your stance, being fueled in this different way, opening to a brand new possibility in life. Watch the magic happen.

How's your energy these days—in your thoughts, words, and what you are doing? Are you hustling too much, frenetic and forcing your way through life? Or are you rocking your rhythm? Ponder what's working and what's not.

Engage (commit)

A nudge. Choose one area to switchfoot today. Small or big. Mix it up. Trust that what you choose is the thing for you to do anew. Remember, it isn't easy to do at first. It will not feel natural or comfortable. But, whew! With practice, it will begin to feel more so and oh, so *good*.

Now, it's your turn. What or who are you beckoned to *commit to*, *connect with*, or *create*—whether in small or big ways?

Share something from this PoP with someone you trust.

Your Word. Write a word that has captured your attention in this PoP.

BE BOLD. BE BRAVE. BE YOU.

Opening the Floodgates

RAISE YOUR VOICE AND SHOUT AN EXUBERANT *YES!* TO YOUR UNIQUE WAYS TO BE AND *DO.*

See new ways to give, serve, and connect with those around you. Uncover and offer your one-of-a-kind gift to those near and far. Share and listen to stories. Take little or big steps. Move with *bistari* and cultivate robust rhythms in your PoPs.

Tend to what is capturing your attention in the struggles of those in your common human family. Explore what is your brave and wholehearted response. As you do, watch for it: the floodgates of *comPASSION* will open. They just will.

You will celebrate differences anew and increase your capacity to love in thought, word, and deed. This shift will be surprising in scope, touching your family, next-door neighbors, good friends whose hearts are breaking … and expand to those far away.

When you are present, with eyes wide open to those around you, you embrace a shared humanity of belonging, *grateFULLY* contemplate your gifts, and eagerly look for opportunities to share what is yours. Here, you are not striving or *trying harder,* but something better moves you.

Compassion is a colossally compelling force.

Take some time to ask—and listen—to compassion's beckoning. Stay rooted in the day-to-day realities of your life. Look for places of inspiration and clarity about what matters most to you.

> To be compassionate is to have a heart that suffers from the misfortune of others because we think of it as our own. We are truly compassionate when we work to remove the misfortune of others. The love of neighbor requires that not only should we be our neighbor's well-wishers, but also their well-doers.
> -Thomas Aquinas

These clues for your next steps will be there.
I have a hunch
they are here
right now.
Sometimes you just need to pause,
adjust your focus,
and look in order to find them.

Be Still (surrender)

Do not tend to doing one thing.
Put thinking aside for now.
Here, you need only be.
Be still.
Be silent.
Be at peace.

ponder (go deeper)

As you listen to "Marchin' On," sung by OneRepublic, consider the ways you want to march today. What are the steps, one foot in front of the other, that you're drawn to take? Write about it all … take it deeper into the soil of your life in your own way.

What captivates you in this section … or in your life? *Ponder* and write about what is beckoning your attention, right here and now.

Reread the quote by Thomas Aquinas in the margin two pages back. What draws you in? What challenges you? Think on and write about the ways you witness the difference between well-wishing and well-doing around and within you.

Engage (commit)

A nudge. Choose one way to be a well-doer (versus a well-wisher). Again, as always — weave this act into the fabric of your life today. Do what you can with what you have and where you are today. *A second nudge.* Practice being still and pondering for a moment before you respond to a point of stress today, an invitation to a function, or a relationship challenge … anything. Do it in real time, in the moment. Trust that clarity about the next thing to do (or not) will come out of this short and sweet moment of attention. Once it comes to you, claim it and do it.

Now, it's your turn. What or who are you beckoned to *commit to, connect with,* or *create* — whether in small or big ways?

Share something from this PoP with someone you trust.

Your Word. Write a word that has captured your attention in this PoP.

BE BOLD. BE BRAVE. BE YOU.

Ruffling Our Feathers

THERE ARE THINGS THAT WHEN WITNESSED, YOU RESPOND TO AUTOMATICALLY, INSTINCTIVELY. YOU JUST DO. *YOU CAN'T NOT.*

If you were to see a child running into a busy street with cars whipping by in rush-hour traffic, you would likely not need to force yourself to shout or do everything possible to reach the little one.

You would do what you could in that moment, likely without a great deal of over-thinking. You would act. *You couldn't not.*

Deepening your belief that you are inextricably interconnected with those in your vast human family transforms your thoughts, your heart, and what you do. Deepening your conviction that those near and far in your human family belong to you and you to them changes the way you see the global realities of poverty, slavery, and exploitation. It becomes nearly impossible to look away.

You can't stand by. You won't stand by. *You won't do nothing.*

My kids have been learning—and in turn, teaching me—about this for years. At school, they are immersed in a community of difference-makers. They tell me about what they are learning regarding the daily choices a person has to make to be a bystander or upstander. These two mindsets are markedly different. A *bystander* is a person who sees someone being mistreated and doesn't do anything. Maybe they look the other way. Their reasons for doing nothing could be because they're afraid, they're in a rush to get to where they're going, or they don't think they are big enough to do anything. These commonplace human pressures lure kids on the playground and adults alike to rush by and look away.

Instead, my kids tell me how they are encouraged to look for opportunities to be *upstanders*. Essentially, an upstander is someone who *wades into the troubles* of their classmates by offering companionship, sticks with them during hard moments, and supports them however they are able. Sometimes this means standing next to a peer who is telling their story. At other times, it involves getting help from a teacher if the situation seems to be bigger than a kid can handle alone.

Simple. And *simply relevant* to what is needed across the planet.

Admittedly, there are times in my life when I'm not an upstander. The difficulty may seem too distant, occurring in a different part of town or halfway around the globe from me. At other times, I see a struggle or injustice, but I look away, because it is too scary, too dark, and too hard to take in—or I don't think there is a way I can make a meaningful difference.

It can be overwhelming and gut-wrenching to see the injustice. Yet, it also feels awful to do nothing, to just stand by or pass by, doing nothing.

Good. I say, *good*. It's *good* that we feel tightness in our jaws or nagging discomfort when we do nothing, pretend, pass by, or walk away. It's *good* that the problem is too big for us to tackle alone and propels us to reach out for our tribe to find ways, together, to do something.

Allowing this very discomfort has changed me in many *EVERYday* ways. In the city in which I live, there are many who stand on street corners, holding signs and asking for help. The less I see these folks as "strangers," the less often I zip off and look away without pausing and doing something … even a *small something*. If I'm on a phone call, I may pause, smile, and wave. Sometimes I make a cup of coffee or hot chocolate to take on the way to school. If I have nothing to give or it's not possible to stop, I may say a prayer of blessing.

You may wonder, "What difference does this really make, waving, smiling, praying, offering a small something in the face of an epic need such as homelessness?" I get it. These very thoughts have slowed, confused, and stopped me. But *I contest* it in my thinking. *I contest* it with everything in me that I need to be a homeless (or other "issue")

The trouble is that once you see it, you can't unsee it. And once you've seen it, keeping quiet, saying nothing, becomes as political an act as speaking out. There's no innocence. Either way, you're accountable.
-Arundhati Roy, Power Politics

expert to do something. *I contest* that only big acts matter. *I contest* insulating myself, keeping at bay uncomfortable feelings of my feathers being ruffled. And yet, there are days I want to just give up … to stop the contesting.

Maybe there have been times when you, too, have wanted to give up instead of contest. If so, it can be tempting to ignore, tolerate, or anesthetize yourself from the pain and discomfort that is present around you. And yet, there are things that beckon for your attention. There are people who beckon for your attention. It takes courage to acknowledge the places that break your heart, to humbly bow your head, observing and tending to the discomfort. This act fuels significant change in your life.

Be willing to be uncomfortable
and
allow your feathers to be ruffled.

It is possible
—and essential—
when you *jOURney* with your tribe.

It is simple, but not easy.

Be Still (surrender)

If discomfort, if a sense of ruffling
has come to light in you, look at it,
and let it go.

If a gripping thought shows up, let it go.
Imagine breathing it out. Exhaling it.
Or picture it in your cupped hands,
and with your big and capable hands,
scoop it up and take it away.

Close your eyes.
Imagine a softening in the tightest parts of you.
Your brow, your jaw, your stomach.
Be here.
Just be.

ponder (go deeper)

Listen to "Love Train," sung by The O'Jays. Really listen to this oldie and goodie, my
friend. If you can allow your mind to wander a bit, to imagine in a childlike way … picture
a train traveling around the world that connects more people than ever before. What does
it look like? Who is on it? Picture yourself on this train, singing your song, doing your thing,
with great grace and joy. *Ponder* and write about your experience here.

What is beckoning your attention from your everyday life right now? Write or speak on a voice memo about what you most desire today, expressing ample details, love, and hope. If these things are lacking, might you reach out to the Sacred, the One, who is with you always, in everything, no matter what? Ask for a glimmer or a flash of whatever you most need.

How comfortable are you to allow moments of discomfort, to really see and sit with the pain and struggle that abounds in the world? Write about it or go for a walk. Consider where you might allow your feathers to be ruffled. Is it in conversations with those in your everyday life, in how you spend your time, in how you spend your money, in boldly exploring your part in a painful reality in the world?

Engage (commit)

A nudge. What is one thing you can do today that you are drawn to, but that you've hesitated exploring before, because it's uncomfortable? This is officially a *feather-ruffling act*, and it can be one that greatly changes you. You rock. You've got this. You're not alone.

Now, it's your turn. What or who are you beckoned to *commit to, connect with,* or *create*—whether in small or big ways?

Share something from this PoP with someone you trust.

Your Word. Write a word that has captured your attention in this PoP.

BE BOLD. BE BRAVE. BE YOU.

Belonging Is Compelling

HERE AND NOW, CONSIDER THE PART YOU ARE DESTINED TO PLAY IN THE WORLD, BECAUSE YOU HAVE A VITAL PART.

Move beyond your comfort zone. Fall in love more and more with your mighty human family.

This connection with people *you call your own* changes things—it will change you. It will open the door for you to unleash more of who you are. It will fan the flame of your one-of-a-kind purpose on the planet.

Perhaps you have been overwhelmed in the past by the plethora of causes or issues that come your way … maybe in a nonstop flood of needs or in a burdensome message that you "*should* do more for others." You may have been burned out with your attempts to respond to such issues in the past. But this is different. The world's challenges, problems, epidemics, and systems of injustice are not so much about *issues*; these issues are really about *people*.

When what you do becomes more focused on *who instead of what*—people instead of issues—things change in a big way. At the heart of these *issues* so often spoken about in the news and in conversation are *people*: mothers, fathers, children, grandparents, brothers, and sisters. They are people with flesh—with legs, arms, eyes, eyelashes, and fingernails. They are people with laughter and longing, dreams and desires.

The purpose and power of this way of seeing one another is that it forges a *compelling connection* that changes your thinking and actions alike. You—we—become bound by belonging.

The boundaries of this belonging are limitless, stable, and connected. This belonging exists between and within countries, races, classes, genders, castes, and on and on.

> This connection with people *you call your own* changes things—it will change you.

It transforms your thinking and your actions … with those nearest and furthest, most similar and most different.

As a global human family, *this is our moment* to stop seeing one another as separate, as other, as strangers. *This is our moment* to stop looking away. *This is our moment* to stop waiting for someone else to do something. *This is our moment* to stop wishing for someone whom we deem more capable or wealthy, someone who seems to have more time, to step up and do something. Our brothers and sisters in our family around the world need us and *we need them*. Many face unimaginable struggle and they feel alone. *This is our moment* to wake up and light it up.

May you discover more of who you are
and what matters most to you.
May you witness with wonder what grows
when you plant your little or big seeds
alongside your unstoppable tribe.

You
were
made
for
this.

If to be feelingly alive to the sufferings of my fellow-creatures is to be a fanatic, I am one of the most incurable fanatics ever permitted to be at large.
-William Wilberforce, slave-trade abolitionist

Be Still (surrender)

Imagine the perfectly contented feeling at the end of a meal.
Good drink, good food.
Life is good.
Cultivate that feeling right here and now.
Be at peace.
Be at rest.
Be.

Ponder (go deeper)

Listen to "Can't Hold Us," sung by Macklemore and Ryan Lewis, featuring Ray Dalton. This is a pumping poetry-song of getting out of bed with profuse purpose and energy, of bringing your superpower of one-of-a-kind juju to the world, and of unstoppably rockin' life together. You might want to get up and move around for this one. If you do, it might be a more breathless pondering and writing sesh of what captured your attention in this song. Just for fun, see if you like the "official music video."

Have you had an experience of meeting a person who deeply impacted and shifted the way you see an issue? If not, imagine how it might change the way it feels to learn about an issue by sitting with someone impacted by that "issue" over a cup of tea in your home.

Where and when have you had the experience of personally connecting with a person who, at a glance, appeared unlike you, but with whom you shared a moment of not-so-otherness and maybe of connection? When have you bumped up against or cultivated interconnection with those most vulnerable, struggling, silenced, or marginalized? If you have had an experience of either, ponder and write about them. Did it feel comfortable, uncomfortable? What did you learn? Are there any bits and pieces you want to draw into your everyday life more (or less) now?

Engage (commit)

A nudge. Take one "issue" that you are intrigued by or care about and make one personal connection around this "cause" today. Think outside the box. For example, if you care about human trafficking, reach out to a company that sells items made by people freed from trafficking and buy a birthday gift for a loved one. Or, fish around a bit to see if there are ways you can further support an organization through spreading the word on social media about what they are doing, through volunteering, or by calling them to make a *real* personal connection.

Now, it's your turn. What or who are you beckoned to *commit to*, *connect with*, or *create*—whether in small or big ways?

Share something from this PoP with someone you trust.

Your Word. Write a word that has captured your attention in this PoP.

BE BOLD. BE BRAVE. BE YOU.

vocations for all

There is an energy,
a trumpet call that beckons you to rise,
to be kindled and set aglow
from within and by those around you.
Here, you will explore what I call:
vocations for all.

These vocations beckon many
—dare I say, all?—of us.
They are simple ways for you to
think, speak, and do
in the midst of your day-to-day life
of work and relationships.

Invite them to elevate, morph,
ignite your vision
for your day-to-day life
and to inform and inspire your next steps.

Warriors

WHAT DO YOU FEEL CURIOUS ABOUT OR COMPELLED TO FIGHT FOR OR AGAINST? WHAT WOULD YOU TRAIN FOR, EVEN TO THE POINT OF EXHAUSTION, AND PERHAPS BEYOND WHAT YOU FEEL CAPABLE OF DOING?

Imagine what or for whom you would be willing to fight. Is it in the context of your everyday, with those you currently serve and love? Or is it about reaching out to a new someone that is capturing your attention and heart?

Do you not know your something to live or fight for yet? Are you still on the hunt? Don't compare, measure, or allow the messages that you are not enough, moving too slow, or going too fast to diminish you. Keep walking, exploring, and trusting—even before you understand it.

I've needed to do the same in many seasons. Though there are lots of things I have yet to understand about this vital vocation, I know that *I am a warrior of love.* A big part of my purpose on the planet is to fight for those in our global human family who are vulnerable and who are struggling in the world due to suffocating challenges of poverty, caste, access to education, and getting their basic needs met. I am committed to fight alongside other mighty warriors who are working on behalf of our sisters and brothers living dangerously in the margins. The more I hear of their crucial strategies for the fight, the more compelled I am to find and invite more to join. Day by day, more come to join this formidable force of fierce warriors.

In all of these vocations, but particularly with the ferocity of this warrior work, the robust rhythms of PoPs are crucial. It is where you can pay attention to things like your focus and fuel.

In this next PoP, listen for that sometimes still, sometimes small, and always present voice of your own heart, of your tribe, and of Spirit. Discern where you are destined to

A true vocation calls us out beyond ourselves; breaks our heart in the process and then humbles, simplifies and enlightens us about the hidden, core nature of the work that enticed us in the first place. We find that all along, we had what we needed from the beginning and that in the end we have returned to its essence, an essence we could not understand until we had undertaken the journey.
-David Whyte,
*Consolations
The Solace,
Nourishment and
Underlying
Meaning of
Everyday Word*

go to battle and with whom, be fueled by your purpose in the midst of the rigors of this vocation, and recover and rest after a fierce fight.

When the dignity, security, and well-being
of those who *BElong* to us
—one or many—
are being challenged,
we
do
something.

We *standTALL*.
We are upstanders.
We shout.
We can't not.

My friend, to be a part of this formidable,
unstoppable army,
you need only claim it.
You
are
a
warrior
of
love.

Be Still (surrender)

Put down your warrior weapons.
No matter how good or necessary they are.
Put them down, here and now.
They are burdensome if never laid down.
Let go of the warrior energy you carry,
your longing to make a difference,
your passion to free, rescue, encourage.
Here, right here.
Just be.
Breathe.
See what confines, what saps, what discourages
and
let
it
go.

ponder (go deeper)

Listen (and watch the video, if you can) to the swelling song, "The World is Ours," sung by Aloe Blacc and David Correy. *Ponder* and write about what captures your attention about lighting up the world, daring to dream, singing your battle cry. Boom, my friend! Let's do this!

What words or ideas from this section are sticking with you? Is it around the question and deepening your clarity about what you want to fight for or against? What would you sweat for, train for, with ferocity and commitment? Or, perhaps it's around the idea of an army, a band of other warriors who oppose injustice in the lives of those near and far?

What are one or two things that you have been exhausted by in your experiences of fighting or working hard for something in life? Something that you see as an integral part of your fuel for life, but if you are propelled too predominantly by it, it gets exhausting and distracting? Think back to an example of it. How can you watch for this subtle fueling issue in the future? If you have an idea about what would be a more sustainable fuel, ponder and write about that, too.

Engage (commit)

A nudge. Dialogue today in your way within your own, private, personal connection with the Sacred or with someone you deeply trust about this vocational invitation to be a warrior. If you have a question in your heart, speak honestly about it. Ask for clarity, focus, energy … whatever you need. Commit to doing one thing today from this exchange of conversation.

Now, it's your turn. What or who are you beckoned to *commit to, connect with,* or *create*—whether in small or big ways?

Share something from this PoP with someone you trust.

Your Word. Write a word that has captured your attention in this PoP.

BE BOLD. BE BRAVE. BE YOU.

peacemakers

SHE DIDN'T HAVE THE *PEACEMAKING* CREDENTIALS YOU WOULD EXPECT.

She brought gifts of bubbles, balloons, and chewing gum on her peacemaking mission to Uganda. She giggled, danced, laughed, and played. She was two years old— our daughter, Sophia.

Ten years ago, our family traveled with an extraordinary group of people. Our destination was Gulu, a village in the north of Uganda, and the Internally Displaced People's (IDP) camps housing nearly two million people in post-war Uganda. Our team was there to listen to, play with, and be a part of life with a bunch of beautiful kids and their families who had been traumatized by growing up in the midst of a brutal civil war. Many were still refugees in their own country and lived in these IDP camps far away from their villages. Even as we arrived, children were missing, the panic of child soldier abductions still striking fear into the hearts of many.

One day, a local leader swept Soph up into her arms and said, "Sophia, our little, yet mighty, Sophia. Do you know what you have done? You have brought hope to us. You have reminded our children that they are not forgotten, that they matter. You make them feel that way because you have traveled so far—halfway around the world—just to be with them. Sophia, you are a peacemaker."

Reminding people that they are not forgotten and that they matter is peacemaking. It makes a mighty difference.

> Reminding people that they are not forgotten and that they matter is peacemaking. It makes a mighty difference.

Claim your vocation as peacemaker. Write it on the business card of your heart. Live it, not only when life is easy, but *BOLDly* when life is hard. Root your life deeper into the soil of peace in regular rhythms of PoPs, where you can connect more often and more deeply with your tribe, with your own heart, with every breath, each day.

Doing something as significant
as peacemaking
—here and now—
is simple.
It is about showing up
and bringing your voice
and vision
to life
and offering it
to the world.

Be Still (surrender)

If it seems war is raging and there is no peace to be had,
pause here.
Rest.
Find solace.
Open your heart.
Invite peace into
the superhighway of your thoughts.
Breathe deeply. Exhale fully.
Be still.
Be.

ponder (go deeper)

Listen to "With My Own Two Hands," sung by Ben Harper, a *beautyFULL* song about kindness, peace, and working together. May it comfort and bring solace to your heart.

What do you bring to the world that is fun, almost effortless, like Sophia's bubbles and gum peacemaking *jOURney* in Uganda? Something that *just happens* when you show up to a place? Write about the ways you share this gift already and how it feels or how you might like to do it a bit more. With whom? Where? When? Dream and design it a bit, my friend, just for fun. *Ponder* and write about what you know and let go of worrying about what you don't know (yet).

What are the areas in the lives of those near and dear to you, or far away, to which you long to bring peace? Before you think on this for too long, pause. Imagine, send, and pray for peace in this very person or place. Trust that there are others who are with you in this. Now, my friend, imagine again: What do you want to do here? Who do you want to invite to join you? Be as specific as you can possibly be. Write this as if it were a screenplay.

Engage (commit)

A nudge. Look for and find one place to be a peacemaker in your day today. It can be small or big, with one you know or a stranger, with one near or far. Dream it and do it.

Now, it's your turn. What or who are you beckoned to *commit to, connect with,* or *create*—whether in small or big ways?

Share something from this PoP with someone you trust.

Your Word. Write a word that has captured your attention in this PoP.

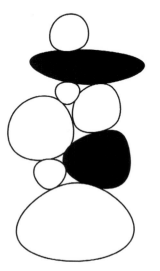

BE BOLD. BE BRAVE. BE YOU.

philanthropists

YOU HAVE GIFTS APLENTY TO GIVE THAT CAN MAKE A MIGHTY DIFFERENCE IN THE WORLD. YOU HAVE MORE THAN YOU THINK YOU HAVE THAT IS OF INEXTRICABLE VALUE TO YOU AND TO THOSE IN YOUR HUMAN FAMILY, NEAR AND FAR.

Generosity feels good. It is part of your purpose on the planet.

Today and together, let's dispute the suggestion that philanthropy is an exclusive club only for those deemed *wealthy*. Today and together, let's dispute that the only thing that matters and makes a difference is giving in "big" ways. Instead, today and together, let's create a movement of philanthropists in which everyone is welcome and all gifts are celebrated.

When we commit to *BEing* and *DOing* life together, we then become part of something big. It then becomes the stuff of movements, powerfully rooted in and growing out of the everyday.

I invite you to try on the hat of philanthropist. *Yes, you.* This sort of philanthropy is about an unrestrained generosity rooted in the reality of your everyday life. It finds ways to share with others the treasure trove of whatever you have and whatever you love. It elevates the way you spend your time and what you talk about with friends. It finds opportunities to travel to places and volunteer with people who captivate your heart. It makes a difference with something as ordinary as shopping, declaring that how and where you shop will be done with a commitment and connection to your sisters and brothers near and far.

> Today and together, let's create a movement of philanthropists in which everyone is welcome and all gifts are celebrated.

This adventure is for you.
It is not for someone else,
for others who seem more privileged,
who seem to have greater bandwidth or capacity,
who seem to be "world-changing types."

You have gifts aplenty to give
that can make a mighty difference in the world.
You have more than you think you have
that is of inextricable value to you
and to those in your human family,
near and far.

It is for you,
for all of us … right here, right now.

The movement that will be unleashed
when we live as generously unrestrained philanthropists
will light up the world.

When we commit
to *BEing* and *DOing*
life together, we
then become part
of something big.
It then becomes the
stuff of movements,
powerfully rooted
in and growing out
of the everyday.

Be Still (surrender)

Whether you feel rich or poor,
with much or little to give ...
whether wearing a hat of philanthropist
is brand new or ancient for you,
let it all go.
Doing and talking time will come.
This is quiet time.
This is being time.
Bask in the silence.
Be here.
Let go. Fill up.

ponder (go deeper)

Listen to "My Wish," sung by Rascal Flatts. As you do, here's a twofold nudge for you to consider. Listen to this song twice. The first time, take it in *all for you*. It is full of sweetness and is a cozy *blanket of blessing* from me to you for your life to be so very *good*. Now, listen to it again. Light a candle. Use this as a meditation, a way to ask for what you need, to send some juju to someone specific, or offer a meditation or prayer for those far off.

Before diving in, just sit for a bit. Let the words, the invitation to wear the hat of a philanthropist wash over you. See if a word or feeling takes root in you around this vocational calling.

Regardless of the amount of money in your bank account, what treasure(s) do you have in your life that would feel good, amazing, *emPOWERing* to share? Be creative and innovative here: think about time, your professional or creative expertise, your personal story, the things you already own that could be shared or loaned to people, conversations throughout your day, or your shopping budget.

Think about the funds you have to give birthday, holiday, and anniversary gifts. Might you give a personal gift to an organization close to the heart of the person you are looking to honor—or around an interest or passion they have, perhaps introducing them to a brand new community of people? Write down some ideas of what would excite you and is doable to start now.

What strikes you about the idea of being generous and philanthropic in your conversations? What do you love to talk about, what really matters to you? What would change if you saw yourself entering into conversations with a treasure to share and on the hunt for treasure to receive from others?

Consider making a donation to a charity you love, making it more personal and connected than it has been in the past. A few ideas:

Call or email the organization and ask if you can deliver the funds in person. Do a little something with or for the folks they serve. Ask if there is a person they serve to whom you might write a personal note with a little bit of inspiration or encouragement—ask if they have any specific recommendations or requests as you do so. Hang a picture of the community of people served by this organization in a place where you see it daily. When you see the picture, send some good juju their way.

If you cannot or are not comfortable personally connecting with the people to whom you're giving funds, play a bit in your imagination. Envision placing your donation directly into the hands of the people receiving those funds. How does this feel?

Whether deepening your connection in-person or in your imagination, remember a time you have been a *recipient*. How did you feel as a *recipient*? Consider how this sort of con-

nection with your own story and with the person to whom you are giving cultivates a sense of being not so different, of being *kindred*. How might seeing the person as a *kindred recipient*, not a distant "beneficiary" receiving a "charitable donation," excite and ignite your generosity and kindle your philanthropy ... whether giving a little or a lot? Ponder and write a bit about this.

Engage (commit)

A nudge. Shift shopping into a philanthropic act one time this week and choose an item that is certified "fair trade" or comes directly from a source that promises to pay its workers well. Or, whether fair trade or not, consider where the item comes from. Before buying it, pause and imagine the hands that crafted it, the eyes focused on making it. Send a prayer, a blessing, or some love to this sister or brother. Hum the "My Wish" song above as you go about your shopping for the many hands that made the items around you. *Bonus Nudge:* Consider committing to this act for thirty days, at which time it just may become a habit.

Now, it's your turn. What or who are you beckoned to *commit to*, *connect with*, or *create*—whether in small or big ways?

Share something from this PoP with someone you trust.

Your Word. Write a word that has captured your attention in this PoP.

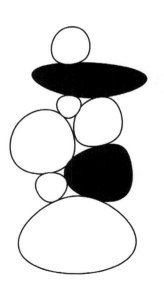

BE BOLD. BE BRAVE. BE YOU.

Hairdressers (stick with me here)

THIS COLLECTIVE VOCATIONAL NUDGE INVITES YOU TO LOOK AROUND AND SEE WHAT IS IN YOUR LIFE RIGHT NOW. RIGHT HERE AND RIGHT NOW.

What simple tools do you wield that can be shared easily with people around you—something that is connected to your job, your passion, or a way of reaching out to those around you that is easy, natural, and currently part of your everyday?

Think about something for which you don't need money, more training, or skills to be able to do. It's something you just do, and it's as easy as breathing.

As you sit with and explore this query, I have a hunch that the following story will inspire you. It is a tale of a global movement that began with a pair of hair-cutting scissors. This account of Joshua Coombes is jaw-dropping in its simplicity and *comPASSION*. Our extraordinary brother Joshua lives and works in the UK and fundamentally believes that *small acts of love greatly matter*. One day, he gathered the tools most natural and familiar to him (a stool, scissors, comb, and a razor), walked out the door of his salon in London, and began offering free haircuts to homeless people on his streets.

> This movement started with Joshua *seeing* the homeless on his streets as people and *looking* at the tools he had at his disposal right then and there. He connected the dots of need and his gifts.

Joshua speaks about the roots of this committed and inspired action: "Hairdressing is how I communicate with people, but anybody, no matter who you are, can do something for nothing, make a difference in your own way. The cool thing, this can be our response to some of the world's problems. Our voice, our hands, our smile are one step away from restoring somebody's hope in humanity."

We all have tools to wield in the world akin to those of Joshua's hairdressing scissors that are simple and have the power to be a part of *restoring hope in humanity*. This is the stuff that adds ceaseless strength to the fabric of life. This is the stuff of significance and belonging. It cultivates and reveals your unique purpose on the planet.

This movement started with Joshua *seeing* the homeless on his streets as people and *looking at* the tools he had at his disposal right then and there. He connected the dots of need and his gifts. Joshua shares that it was the nagging questions and his own sense of powerlessness that ultimately nudged him to begin.

Overwhelm didn't stop him. His destiny and next steps—just like yours—resided right next to his feelings of helplessness. He found the gold in the very place of discomfort. The struggles of homelessness around him did not *deter* him, but *propelled* him.

As he walked, one step at a time, day after day, Joshua began capturing the attention of those around him. One by one, others have joined him. When two changemakers with gifts in compelling cultural "storymaking" (entrepreneur, Dave Burt, and musician, Matt Spracklen) heard about what he was up to, they reached out to Joshua. These three gelled—they clicked. They began to do together what they could not have done solo. They now call themselves a *band of brothers* and have started a global campaign called #DoSomethingForNothing. They say that this movement is fundamentally about linking influencers around the world through social media, spreading love around the world, and connecting the *haves* with the *have nots*.

Today, Joshua is in the salon less and traveling around the world more, speaking about this mighty global campaign with simple roots in his own backyard. Joshua's path has been uncharted and unplanned. But, one step and leap at a time, it has grown far beyond where it was when he started on the day he picked up his hairdresser's tools and walked out his door to offer a free haircut.

In the face of such epic problems … start here.
See your helplessness, your overwhelm.
Don't be deterred, but be propelled
by the things
that seem bigger than you.

Don't wait for someone else with more skills, more money,
more _____ (fill in the blank with the thoughts that stop you from acting),
to do something.

Start where you are with what you have and make your way.
You can iterate, change, morph over time.
But starting is the key.

Your steps will lead to unplanned places.
It is always so.
Get to stepping.

There is no stopping,
no end,
no limit to the possibilities available
when we start and carry on,
together.

Be Still (surrender)

Helplessness and overwhelm.
Excitement and possibility.
Worry and anxiety.
Strategizing and thinking.
Set these and any other thoughts
aside that are floating or bombarding.
Let them go.
Soften. Gently smile.
Inhale and exhale big and fully.
Breathe.
Just breathe.
Be.
Just be.
Stay here and be.

ponder (go deeper)

Listen to (and watch the video, if you can) "Fresh Eyes," sung by Andy Grammar. What is beckoning your attention in this poetry-song, in your life, around this notion of how it is we look at and see one another? *Ponder* and write about it here.

What tools do you have that you can pick up and share with ease and joy? What does it look like and who are you serving? Who are you working with … or are you on your own? This is such an important invitation, dear friend. It's for you. Take it in and pay attention to what thoughts and ideas come to you within this story that connects to your story, your life, here and now.

Invite the Sacred to speak, to whisper, to nudge you towards your next step today. Ask the burning questions in you. Share any worries or wonders. Be real, here, in this place of great Love and affirmation.

Engage (commit)

A nudge. Hop online and explore the #DoSomethingForNothing campaign. Watch some of their stirring videos. Take one nugget that inspires you and do something about it today: explore, play, act.

Now, it's your turn. What or who are you beckoned to *commit to*, *connect with*, or *create*—whether in small or big ways?

Share something from this PoP with someone you trust.

Your Word. Write a word that has captured your attention in this PoP.

BE BOLD. BE BRAVE. BE YOU.

Bridge-Builders

CULTIVATING A TRIBE WITHIN WHICH THERE IS PRISMATIC DIVERSITY AND COURAGEOUSLY MOVING AWAY FROM SURROUNDING OURSELVES WITH SAMENESS IS TREMENDOUSLY SIGNIFICANT AND POWERFUL.

Arms of bridge-building hospitality are powerful and far-reaching. This way of thinking and acting seeks to reach not only those who are familiar or in your comfort zone, but those who are wildly and beautyFULLY diverse.

I believe we can change the world if we start listening to one another again. Simple, honest, human conversation... Human conversation is the most ancient and easiest way to cultivate the conditions for change–personal change, community and organizational change, planetary change. If we can sit together and talk about what's important to us, we begin to come alive.
-Margaret Wheatley, *Turning to One Another*

It's about celebrating difference and finding places of similarity that take your breath away, filling life with more palpable purpose and connection than ever before.

In our world today, most of our political systems are split and broken and many people—regardless of nationality, race, gender, or generation—are struggling to make it through each day. The challenges you have experienced may look or sound different from another's struggles, but, oh my, we are more similar than different. I am here to offer both a gentle nudge and a caffeine-filled jolt to vehemently oppose the tendency to erect walls built by bricks of fear, shame, judgment, ignorance, distrust, and misunderstanding, to beckon you to cultivate curiosity, celebrate connection in unexpected places, and fiercely commit to honoring differences.

Whew. That's a lot, right? And yet, it's simple. My kids have taught me over the years about the difference between being an upstander and a bystander. They remind us to reach out, not to look away, and to do our part. This is the sort of wisdom wee ones have. They know this to be true. Sometimes as we grow older, we forget.

Let's *REmember* together. Here and now.

To do so now is a crucial commitment in the context of humanity, in a big global way, as well as a deeply personal one. It is rooted in the real, within the quotidian, ordinary acts of going to school, working, and raising children.

Every day, you encounter people and places in social media, in the news, at work, in your neighborhood, and within your family that may seem strange, scary, too much *this* or not enough *that* as you go about your life. Imagine if, beginning with you, more and more people claim the work of bridge-building and endeavor to fiercely find ways and places to connect, despite differences and seemingly deep division. This vocation may lead you to one near and dear: your spouse, your child, a family member, friend, neighbor … or to one distant and different, due to culture, race, or religion.

As a bridge-builder, the next time you encounter a moment of difference, or of *otherness*, lean in, curiously ask questions, and really listen to and share with one another.

Claiming and crafting
this bridge-building vocation
will reorient your gaze and your gifts.
It is nothing less than *REVolutionary.*
Your thoughts, words, and actions
may be distinctively different.
Your actions will ripple out and grow from you,
making the world a bit brighter,
a bit better.

To do so now is a crucial commitment in the context of humanity, in a big global way, as well as a deeply personal one. It is rooted in the real, within the quotidian, ordinary acts of going to school, working, and raising children.

Be Still (surrender)

A hopeful future
is rooted in peace.
Peace and pause within.
Peace, peace.
Breathe.
Be.

ponder (go deeper)

Listen to "One Tribe," sung by Black Eyed Peas. Get up and move around, dance, spin, and take in this epic and amazing connection with a tribe of many that is here for you right here and now. As you sit, sing, or dance, what is capturing your attention in this poetry-song? *Ponder* and write it down.

What is going on in your own life today that connects to the stories of bridge-building? What word or phrase about this idea stuck with you? Chew on those words and make room for the seeds of your story to grow here, today.

How might seeing yourself as a bridge-builder impact your closest relationships with family and friends? How about strangers you pass in your daily life? How about when you travel or engage with people in faraway lands? Imagine how it will feel to increase the ways in which you embrace curiosity, even celebration, when you encounter a place of difference. Write about one such moment. Include juicy details in your description.

Engage (commit)

A nudge. Choose one person with whom to connect today—near or far, intimate friend or distant stranger. If nothing comes to you right away, go on the hunt for an opportunity to practice being a bridge-builder in your way.

Now, it's your turn. What or who are you beckoned to *commit to, connect with,* or *create*—whether in small or big ways?

Share something from this PoP with someone you trust.

Your Word. Write a word that has captured your attention in this PoP.

BE BOLD. BE BRAVE. BE YOU.

Explorers

THE JOURNEY OF LIFE WILL BRING MOMENTS IN WHICH YOU FEEL AS THOUGH YOU ARE NAVIGATING UNCHARTED TERRITORIES. THEY WILL COME. THEY ALWAYS DO.

It can take great courage and the adventure can be thrilling. Consider that claiming the vocation of an explorer might just free you from the burden of needing to know where you are going and how you are getting there.

Rooted in Latin *explorare*, the word "explore" means to "investigate, search out, examine." Rarely, if ever, is seeing the whole path part of the quest. The exploration most often involves regions yet unfamiliar. Sometimes there are maps to consult; other times, the lands are brand new. Either way, navigating undiscovered terrains is part of the work of an explorer. It is to be expected. It is normal. Will there be unfamiliar places? Yes. Will there be unknown places? Of course. Will there be uncomfortable places? Most definitely. Though sometimes challenging, these conditions do not disqualify you; in fact, they are evidence that you are living your calling as an explorer.

Another important nudge for the road: As you continue to explore, you may or may not discover things that you deem significant. Not to worry. Keep walking. Keep exploring. Discoveries don't add to the sparkling worth of who you are.

There are always new possibilities around the bend. Keep expanding your purpose on the planet, your tribe, and the ways in which *inspired doing* lights you up. Life as an explorer has no end, and it is never hum-drum or boring. It gives you a reason to get up in the morning. On some days, it takes everything you've got to stay focused and keep fueled for the rigors of life. Exploring can be hard work and can tax the body, mind, heart, and soul. You may become travel-weary in the days to come. But, my intrepid-explorer-friend, you have essentials for the road as you cultivate your own PoP practices—times to contemplate and commit to action that is fueled from deep within

> Keep expanding your purpose on the planet, your tribe, and the ways in which *inspired doing* lights you up.

you. Take them with you wherever you go. They are vital and all the more crucial in rigorous days that find you traversing uncharted territories.

Keep going.
Persevere.
Be *COURAGEous.*

In it all, may you know
that being an explorer is not about
discovering,
doing, or
daring
more
to
be
more.

Grow your roots
in the indisputable,
uncontested, the
unshakable:
You have glittering gifts.
You matter.
You are loved.
You are not alone – not now, not ever.

Be Still (surrender)

Here we are.
You may have more questions you want answered,
more clarity you need,
more you want to know and understand.
But, as we've done throughout this *jOURney*,
in this moment,
let your brow relax,
your jaw loosen.
Remember this is not up to you entirely.
You do not need to force, strive, or push.
Let these things go.
Be.
Breathe.
Soften.
Let go of the burdens.
Open to what you most need.
Just be.

ponder (go deeper)

Listen to "A Beautiful Day," sung by the amazing India Arie. This song is all about being explorers, *grateFULLness*, and elegant ease. *Ponder* and write about what rises within you as you listen to her song-poetry.

How might claiming this vocation of an explorer shift your expectation that you need to know everything all the time? How might it reduce your sense of worry and increase peace when you find yourself in uncharted places, in the land of the not-yet-understood?

Are there any bits of your life, whether in relationships, work, or your own clarity about your purpose on the planet, that burden you to see more clearly? *Ponder* and consider if there is another way, a lighter and freer way, to navigate uncharted and undiscovered territories.

Engage (commit)

A nudge. Commit to one thing you are most keen to explore, without the burden or pressure of needing to understand or see the whole path. One person or place or thing that is drawing you to come and see, to pay attention. Write it down. Do one thing today to be the intrepid explorer that you are.

Now, it's your turn. What or who are you beckoned to *commit to*, *connect with*, or *create*—whether in small or big ways?

Share something from this PoP with someone you trust.

Your Word. Write a word that has captured your attention in this PoP.

BE BOLD. BE BRAVE. BE YOU.

4

[blazing]

being on fire. being excited. eager. zealous. ardent. burning brightly and with great heat. having a force of tremendous intensity or fever. gleaming with bright lights, bold colors.

taking flight

It's time to leap, soar, and light up the world.
You were made for this.

This is your
—this is our—
purpose on the planet.
Hold your head high,
your eyes bright, direct, and fierce.
Grab a hand and leap *BOLDly* and
COURAGEously.

Leap and fly.
Live ablaze
and let's light up the world,
together.

Claim & Leap

IMAGINE THAT THIS ADVENTURE HAS BROUGHT YOU TO THE EDGE OF A CLIFF.

The vista from this vantage point is spectacular, unlike anything you've seen before. As you stand at the edge, with the parachute strapped to your back, you know it:

It is time to leap.

Your heart pounds, your breath is short. You long for the leap, to feel the wind on your skin as you fly free and unfettered. But it is not easy. You have never leapt from this height before. You know that you must jump for the 'chute to open. The terror and the thrill make for a racing heart.

Thrum-Thrum. Thrum-Thrum. Amidst the tumult of your racing heart and the whipping of the wind, something catches your eye. As you look to the left and right, you see it. It is not *something*, but *someone* … a lot of *someones*, in fact.

The cliff ledge is lined with others, and more are coming. They have been *jOURney-ing* and exploring, taking small and big steps, leading them to this cliff's edge. Just like you. With you.

POP

THIS BONUS POP WILL SET THE STAGE FOR YOU TO SEE, REALLY SEE, THE STUNNING PANORAMA OF YOUR JOURNEY THUS FAR.

It will quiet your heart and your mind to see and listen in that soulful way to take in the beauty and courage that is you. Right here, right now.

Be Still (surrender)

Whew.
Jumping from a cliff, with a parachute strapped to your back...
these are audacious and exhilarating imaginings, aye?
We'll return to them in a bit.
For now, my dear friend,
take this time for silence and stillness.
Let go of the possibilities and conundrums,
the things known or unknown.
Excitement or fear.
Be here.
Breathing.
Being.

ponder (go deeper)

Listen to (and watch the video, if you can) "Wavin' Flag – Celebration Mix," sung by K'NAAN. This is the final jam to rock to in our time together on this journey. Celebrate this PoP. Get up and move around, dance, spin, and take in this epic and amazing connection with a tribe of many that is here for you right here and now. As you sit, sing, or dance, what is capturing your attention in this poetry-song? *Ponder* and write it down.

Think back to the shared vocations. Which ones most beckon you to claim them, as if they are written below your name on a business card? Mark the vocations that most compel and excite you. Add ones that call to you that aren't listed here. Dream big here. Without shoulds. Free from fear.

Warrior
Peacemaker
Philanthropist
Bridge-builder
[Your hairdresser-tool]
Explorer

The ones you marked are you. This is your call. This is who you are and what you do.

Engage (commit)

A nudge. Pick one of your vocational choices above and write a job description of how *you* do this work. Give this way of life some empowering details. Imagine it. Write what you know and what you dream of … and let go of what you don't yet know. *Do one thing* today connected to this inspiring "job description."

Now, it's your turn. What or who are you beckoned to *commit to*, *connect with*, or *create*—whether in small or big ways?

Share something from this PoP with someone you trust.

Your Word. Write a word that has captured your attention in this PoP.

BE BOLD. BE BRAVE. BE YOU.

Panoramic View

YOU'VE DONE IT ... COMPLETED YOUR FINAL POP! THERE HAVE BEEN FORTY POPS, PLUS A BONUS EXPERIENCE, FOR YOUR UNFOLDING STORY TO DEEPEN, EMERGE, AND GROW. YOU'VE HAD THE OPPORTUNITY TO KINDLE THE FIRE OF YOUR DREAMS, HOPES, AND PURPOSE ON THE PLANET.

As we near the end of this *jOURney*, amidst the energy of this, blazing with potential and the promise of next steps and future leaps, I invite you to take a moment.

Now, my friend, reflect back on your PoPs. If you've kept a journal, flip through its pages for more insight. Look for patterns and possibilities that have emerged out of these PoPs. Expect to be surprised. Don't force, try harder, or stress. Let go. Trust. Play.

What do you see, sense, hear? What words, ideas, or ahas? What people or places? What struggles, joys, longings, or hopes? What has emerged and popped out of the soil? What has come to life in you? What serves as kindling, lighting you up from within? What things do you want to do—differently or anew? This is the gold. Come and see.

> Expect to be surprised. Don't force, try harder, or stress. Let go. Trust. Play.

Zoom out the lens. Imagine you're a bird flying or have a parachute strapped to your back, and gaze down at the landscape of your life from this *jOURney*, perhaps found in the pages of your journal and in your unique PoPs. Or, as if this book were a film, allow your mind to rewind and show you a picture of the different moments and scenes you've lived and experienced thus far.

Wear that explorer's hat. Look for new terrains to discover as you distill your story. In the days to come, it will continue to morph, change, and grow. But what do you see here and now, on this very day?

Whatever emerges, give it some space to breathe. What is something you can do to sit with it, to cultivate it, to explore it further? Go for a walk. Write about it. Draw or paint it. Sing or dance it. Do whatever you desire—no more, no less.

Allow the brilliance of *your* story to flourish and shine.

Journey Landmark

THIS STACK OF STONES IS CALLED A *CAIRN*, WITH SCOTTISH GAELIC ORIGINS, MEANING "HEAP OF STONES."

An old Scottish Gaelic blessing is *Cuiridh mi clach air do chàrn*, meaning, "I'll put a stone on your stone."

It has unique purposes and uses around the globe, often dating back to prehistoric times. In North Africa, they are called a *kerkours*, in Portual *moledros*, in Mongolia, *ovoos*, and *inuksuks* by the Inuit peoples. One of the ways cairns have been and still are used is to erect them as landmarks, which is what I invite you to do now.

Choose three words that describe this moment of your journey. Look back to the Panoramic View for the themes you saw. If you need to, flip back to the My Word sections of the PoPs that were the most impactful for you. Close your eyes and sit for a moment to see if your three words come to you. Play a bit here. Explore.

As the three words come to you, create a landmark for your journey using the stack of stones. Write your three words in the large white stones of the cairn.

My friend, this is *your* landmark for this moment on the journey. It is unique to you, something you can return to in the days to come to remember this spot, this very place.

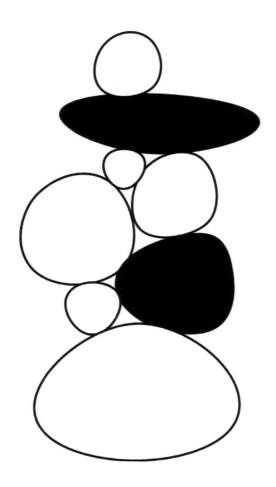

Keep at It

CONSIDER WHAT HAVE BEEN YOUR FAVORITE ELEMENTS OF THE POPS. DO YOU WANT TO CONTINUE TO PRACTICE YOUR POPS IN DAILY LIFE?

Is it something you plan to do at the same time(s) each day and/or on-the-fly, in response to the stressors and challenges that arise in day-to-day living?

Feel free to use the framework—*Be Still, Ponder,* and *Engage*—as a starting point and freely tweak it to make it your own. Consider that time to *Be Still* means not thinking, strategizing, or planning, but just *BEing;* time to *Ponder*—to reflect, to contemplate—represents going a level or two deeper into your life, panning for the gold and the glimmer within you; and time to *Engage*—to work these moments of stillness and pondering into your life—allows you to explore and experiment, doing things to see what's working and what's not, in connection with your tribe and companioned by your own relationship with the Sacred. Remember that whatever you do, never go it alone.

A daily rhythm of PoPs will nurture a life that is solid and whole, lit up with a glow that is unique to you. As your PoP practice grows, you'll find yourself using these PoPs spontaneously when life throws you a curveball—which all of us experience at one time or another. Look for ways to take the triggers that come your way during the day—worry, fear, opportunity, decisions to make, relationships to negotiate, people you love who are in pain and in need of support—and take these into a spur-of-the-moment PoP.

Right now, as you envision your own persistent PoPs, write about how and when you will continue this practice, including as many details as possible to direct and inspire you to solidify your PoPs and make them your own.

A nudge. Share your practice and intention with at least one person in your tribe.

> A daily rhythm of PoPs will nurture a life that is solid and whole, lit up with a glow that is unique to you.

(Not) The End

AS WE APPROACH THE VERY END OF THIS LEG OF OUR *JOURNEY* TOGETHER, THIS IS NOT THE END.

We have much left to do, together. That's good news. So keep that seatbelt fastened, dear friend. You're gonna need it.

Here and now, I invite you to partake of one last imagining that has its roots in each day of this journey. This dream is becoming more real by the moment. It is real-time. It is here and now.

You sit listening to the sea of humanity, to your sisters and brothers, near and far. You hear lilting voices, languages you do not understand. You see lands that are unfamiliar, people with whom you lock eyes. When they see you, they smile, greet you, and offer tea. Their eyes twinkle, sparkle, and beckon you to come closer, to bring others with you, to not look away. They invite you to come and sit, to rest, to feast with them.

You say yes. You let yourself go and *enJOY* the feast. *You can't not.* It's too *good.* In their company, you feel less fear and loneliness ... *plentiful peace, flourishing freedom, herculean hope,* and *limitless love* are here. Right here, right now. In you and in those around you.

You hear a song ... a mighty and unstoppable melody of voices is coming together. In the din, you hear it: the free, beautiful shouting of your own voice. And, among these many, you feel it: you *BElong.*

You have become a vital part of a mighty community of many others, who wade into the deep and dark places of the world, carrying the torch of hope as you go. Together, you are peacemakers, not fettered by fear of difference, the unknown, or the unfamiliar. You keep it real, speak about and listen to what really matters to one another,

You have become a vital part of a mighty community of many others, who wade into the deep and dark places of the world, carrying the torch of hope as you go.

live *BEloved*, and fervently vow to *be love*. You are humble warriors of love and justice who *BElong* to one another.

Right here, right now, as a tribe, you celebrate one another's unique and one-of-a-kind destinies that are unstoppably growing and flourishing with jaw-dropping beauty.

> You create things that make life better for those near and far. You are a tribe of makers who make a difference ... you are a *kula* of changemakers.

Together, you live your big dreams, the ones you have dared to hope and claim as real and true. You pick up the tools that are yours to wield with innovative brilliance. You create things that make life better for those near and far. You are a tribe of makers who make a difference ... you are a *kula* of changemakers.

You bask in the thrill of the thrumming of your hearts on this adventure that continues on ... each and every day. This is a way of life that is yours till your last breath. This adventure has no end, and there is always more exploring to be done.

This tribe won't wait to hoot and holler its cheers until things are all figured out. Collectively, you let go and boldly celebrate and trust that your next steps will appear at just the right time and in ways that are more than you could have thought to dream of or imagine.

Together, you dare to rest, to play, to let go, to dance, to sing, to feast, to envision, to plan for, and to pour yourselves into work that you love, that sustains your lives, and that enables you to provide for those you love. You are known as those who walk the planet with unrestrained generosity, a mighty community of *EXTRAvagant* philanthropists, from the kindergarteners to the elders, from the richest to the poorest, from the haves to the have-nots. You see and claim that this is your human birthright and live it more fully every day.

Your community's gratitude is inexhaustible. It is oceanic. You have plenty and are plenty. You cherish the beauty, the hope, the *enough-ness* that is here now. You are buoyed; your loads are lightened. And about those loads—you carry these burdens together. You are burden-bearers for one another in the dark and light moments of life.

You live humbly and unrestrained in your interdependence as a tribe. You bask in a steady stream of conversation with each other, as trusted soul friends. These conversations extend to include more and more of those in your human family, and with the always-with-and-for-you, Spirit.

Wow. Now, it's time to take a breath.

What's coming next is so important, dear one.

Listen. Do you hear it? The tribe of your human family has gathered and is cheering *you* on. Celebrating *you*. Cheering for *you*. Seeing *your* freedom, courage, *comPASSION*, and your fierce and unstoppable commitment to *be love*.

I am in this crowd, shouting rowdy *hurrahs* for *you*.

We wildly *whoop your* name. We rise to our feet and stomp a boisterous standing ovation for *you*. We revel in who *you* are, who *you* have become, and who *you* are yet to be. We are ecstatic and ready to keep leaping and to light up the world with *you*. The cause of our thunderous praise is crystal clear. You rock and *you are ablaze*.

So, my wondrous and extraordinary friend, buckle your seatbelt.

It's only just begun.

With a heart full-to-the-brim of great love and hope …

xo

Sarah DT

[glowing]

emitting warmth. showing radiance.
being rich and warm in color.
shining with an intense heat.

the jOURney continues

We hope this journey
has held up a mirror so that you now see yourself
and the world with new eyes,
has illuminated a long-held passion
or a brand new one,
has encouraged and inspired you,
has ignited you with a vision and strategy
for increased connection,
has energized you with a sense of
your one-of-a-kind purpose on the planet,
has filled you to the brim with curiosity,
has elevated the dignity of all,
including your own,
and
has lit you up with
hope,
love,
and joy ...
from this day forward.

You belong here.
We belong to each other.
Let's standTALL together and light up the world.

Join the Seeds Kula Collective

WELCOME, DEAR FRIEND. IF YOU'VE EVER WONDERED HOW ONE PERSON COULD POSSIBLY MAKE A DIFFERENCE JUST BY SHOWING UP EXACTLY AS THEY ARE—WELCOME TO THE SEEDS *KULA* COLLECTIVE!

We invite you to learn, expand, link arms for change, to live ablaze and light up the world. You belong here.

We are a collective of everyday people who are committed to light up the world so that a mighty difference can be made *together*. We do what we do because we believe that we belong to each other and that each and every person matters. We passionately work to make an indelible dent in global human rights *and* in one another's day-to-day lives.

We connect individuals, non-profits, government agencies, or businesses, in order to increase the ability of each to make a unique and significant impact. *Everyone* has something of value to share with others—whether time, money, voice, or purpose.

There are things for which we have each been destined that we cannot do alone. Step by step, arm in arm, we are creating a well-worn path of inspired vision and action, making mighty contributions, and offering our gifts in response to some of the world's greatest challenges.

In our community, you can rest, pause, take a breath, you can *be*. Be you.

Listen for the trumpet call to rise, to leap, to be inspired from within and by our people to say *YES!* We promise, this community will light you up. You—we—will never be the same.

You belong here.
We belong to each other.
Let's *standTALL* together and light up the world.

Visit bit.ly/SeedsComm to sign up for stories from around the world to inspire and ignite

seedsofexchange.org | connect@seedsofexchange.org

Facebook & Instagram @SeedsOfExchange

grateFULL

WITHOUT Y'ALL, MY TREASURED AND TRUSTED TRIBE, THIS BOOK WOULD NOT BE ... MY TOUR GUIDE, MY LOVE IN AND FOR ALL OF LIFE, JESUS.

My extraordinary and treasured family, you are my roots: Mom & Dad, Beks Vashti Abraham E, Liz T, Aunt Deb & the Berks, Grandpa John & Grandma Marion, Grandpa & Grandma Tracy, Momma Sue & Nana, Cody & Mel & the D's, the Carlson Crew.

This book was crafted, propelled, and buoyed within a most-extraordinary collective of sistahs and brothas, my *book kula*. Donna Mazzitelli (merrydissonancepress.com), on paper, you are an editor, but, in reality, you have been part midwife, sage, teacher, shepherd, and *anam cara* (a Gaelic term for "soul friend"). You are a glittering gift. Astrid Koch (astridkoch.com), thank you for being a part of launching this story into the world with jaw-dropping beauty, clarity, and impact. 'Cuz that's just what you do. Andrea Costantine (communityforthesoul.com), you have been a champion and guide of this project since its inception, and I'm ecstatic and thankful for your part in crafting the look and feel within *Live Ablaze* to be one of experiential beauty, connection, and adventure. Polly Letofsky and Susie Schaefer (mywordpublishing.com), your fierce companioning and extraordinary expertise has made this book journey one of far greater ease, joy, and excellence than it would have been on my own. Danielle Norris (sovenco. com), not only were you the first person on the planet to read this manuscript, but your heartbeat to align strategy, impact, and humanity has been pivotal in this project and for Seeds. Amy K Wright (amykwright.com), you are tenacious in your commitment to tell stories well, and I am over-the-moon-grateful for your part in this tale. J Renae Davidson (jcreative.us), thank you for the rockin' photograph sesh—you have such a gift. Rachael Jayne and Datta Groover and Tom Bird (grooverseminars.com & tombird.com), your invitation, collaboration, and support catapulted this book into being.

My sistahs and brothas, for life: Susan & the C's, Aya & the S's, Nil H, JJ & the C's, Amy & the B's, Kathleen & the V's, Rochelle & the R's, Raquel & the PS's, Papa Jim P, Lisa & the S's, Erin & the E's, Q & the S's, Grant K, Josh D, Ryan B, Christy & the G's Raju & Samita & the S's, Hakan G, Hannah B, Ruth B, Pabitra B, Sangeeta A, Anjila SK, Jaimala G, Delta D, Astrid K, VKP, Dom DR, Helberth R, Anne E, Alexis N, Lydia D, Winter W, Aliyah J, Vaun S, Bill & Jane R, Lil', Stu S, Lima & Malika A, Marcellina & the O's, Godee & the M's, Anna & the W's, Rose & the O's, Kel & My Joe C, Fatouma & Ibrahim & the AY's, Nicole & Phil & the A's, Bill Z, Barb Y, Meg & the S's, Jorge C, Kate H. You have each played a real, true, and vital part in this story.

To the most-amazing changemakers and storytellers of *The True Cost* film team (truecostmovie.com), Shima Akhter, *Resurface* film team (resurfacethemovie.com), Operation Surf (amazingsurfadventures.biz/programs/operation-surf), Van Curaza, Bobby Lane, Vedran Smailović, Christina Noble and the Christina Noble Children's Foundation (cncf.org), and the *band of brothers* of the #DoSomethingForNothingCampaign, Joshua Coombes, Dave Burt, and Matt Spracklen.

And, the finale of my thanks is to my beloveds. Soph and Micah, you two inspire me to my core, and the little people you are makes my heart thrum with more love than I ever imagined possible. Bran, you have been a part of each and every step of this journey, offering your clear-sighted and rock-solid vision, cheering me on unceasingly. You have been a real-life picture of fierce and extravagant love. I love you three.

Let gratitude be the pillow upon which you kneel to say your nightly prayer.
-Maya Angelou

Read More and Journey on

grow...contribute...commit...standTall...belong.

Live ablaze
AND LIGHT UP THE WORLD

SARAH DAVISON-TRACY

IF YOU'VE EVER WONDERED HOW ONE PERSON COULD POSSIBLY MAKE A DIFFERENCE JUST BY SHOWING UP EXACTLY AS THEY ARE–WELCOME!

Link arms, learn, expand for change, and light up the world with us. One step at a time, you will uncover more of who you are and what matters most to you. You will be fueled for a life that is peace-making, bridge-building, and change-making.

You may feel more-than-ready, eager to receive this invitation at this very moment, or you may feel that you don't yet have energy for such a life. Wherever you are, whatever you are doing right here and now, you are in just the right spot. As we journey together, the glow of hope, peace, and love will stoke the flames of a life far beyond what you ever dared to dream.

LiveAblazeBook.com